D1582969

NUNEATON TO LOUGHBOROUGH

and Ashby-de-la-Zouch to Derby

Vic Mitchell and Keith Smith

MP Middleton Press

Front cover: A fine example of railway restoration was recorded at Market Bosworth on 16th March 2013. No. 30585 is a 2-4-0WT, which had worked on the Southern Railway for much of its career. (J.Whitehouse)

Back cover: Railway Clearing House map for 1947.

ACKNOWLEDGEMENTS

We are very grateful for the assistance received from many of those mentioned in the credits, also from N.Allsop, R.Bulmer (Shackerstone Railway Society Ltd), A.J.Castledine, G.Croughton, G.Gartside, D.Harris, A.C.Hartless, J.Horne, C.M.Howard, N.Langridge, B.Lewis, D.K.Jones, J.Nash, Mr D. and Dr S. Salter, T.Walsh and, in particular, our always supportive families.

Published July 2017

ISBN 978 1 910356 08 1

© Middleton Press, 2017

Production Editor Deborah Esher
Typesetting & design Cassandra Morgan
Cover design Matthew Esher

Published by
      Middleton Press
      Easebourne Lane
      Midhurst
      West Sussex
      GU29 9AZ
Tel: 01730 813169
Email: info@middletonpress.co.uk
www.middletonpress.co.uk

Printed and bound by CPI Group (UK) Ltd, Croydon, CR0 4YY

CONTENTS

INDEX

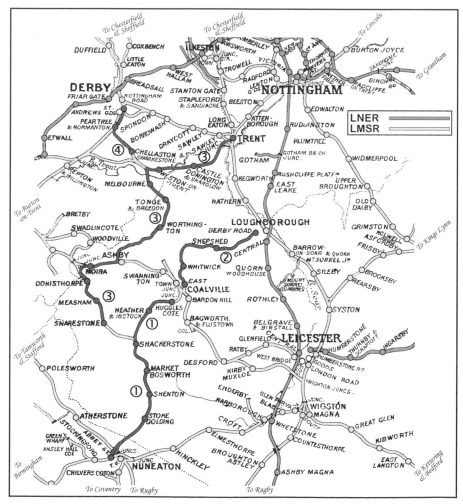

Ia.   The 1947 Railway Clearing House map has received the numbers of the Contents section of this album, together with black lines to show the routes herein. They were not all linked operationally. The copy on the back cover is unaltered.

GEOGRAPHICAL SETTING

The majority of the lines herein were built in Leicestershire, but at the western edge of the area they pass in and out of Derbyshire. The deviation of the boundary is shown by a dotted line on map Ia.

The high ground of the district is between Loughborough and Moira. Its springs give rise to the River Sence, which flows south near Shackerstone, and some streams that run north into the River Trent. This was once an important commercial artery running east-west across England, with many canals connected to it. The River Soar, from the south, and the River Erewash, from the north, join the River Trent, near Trent station. It then runs into the River Humber, which runs to the east coast at Hull.

South of the Trent and north of Coalville were a number of productive coal deposits in an area of mainly sandstone. South of Shepshed, a substantial water reservoir was completed in 1906, but on 11th February 1957 it was subjected to a serious earthquake (Richter scale 5). The damage to it and the district was minimal, luckily.

The main coalfield was within a 10 mile square, centred on Ashby-de-la-Zouch.

The maps are to the scale of 25ins to 1 mile, with north at the top, unless otherwise indicated.

HISTORICAL BACKGROUND

Nuneaton was served by the Rugby to Tamworth line of the London & North Western Railway from 1847. The Midland Railway reached the town from Birmingham in 1864. The LNWR had worked from Coventry since 1850 and Hinckley from 1862.

The Ashby & Nuneaton Joint Committee of the MR and LNWR operated the route between those places from 1st September 1873 (goods earlier), running via both Snarestone and Coalville. The route through the latter had been part of an 1833 mineral tramway. The line through Ashby and Moira to Burton-on-Trent had been opened to passengers by the MR on 1st March 1849. Freight was conveyed from 1848.

Burton had received the Birmingham & Derby Junction Railway in 1839. Loughborough and Trent were served by the Midland Counties Railway from 1840. This became the MR in 1844. From Trent Junction, there was the 1839 line to Nottingham and the 1847 MR route to Long Eaton and the North of England.

The MR opened their line through Castle Donington to Trent on 6th December 1869. Its extension west to Repton came into use on 3rd November 1873.

The MR ran south from Melbourne Junction, near Peartree, to reach Melbourne on 1st September 1868, Worthington on 1st October 1869 and Ashby on 1st January 1874.

The line north from Coalville to Loughborough (Derby Road) was authorised under an Act of 16th July 1874 and was opened by the Charnwood Forest Railway on 16th April 1883. This company, along with the MR, LNWR and others, became part of the London Midland & Scottish Railway in 1923. The latter formed most of the London Midland Region of British Railways upon nationalisation in 1948.

Closures began early regarding passenger services. They ceased between Ashby and Derby and between Worthington and Trent on 22nd September 1930, as they did on the Chellaston link line. Nuneaton to Moira followed on 13th April 1931, along with Coalville to Loughborough. Through freight closures took place mainly in 1955-65. The dates for sidings and goods yards appear in the captions. The route west from Trent Junction to Burton was still in use in 2017, as was the line through Coalville and Moira, although these stations had been long closed.

The southern part of the route through Chellaston closed to through freight in 1973. The northern part reopened to serve two new stations at Sinfin on 4th October 1976. They were closed on 17th May 1993, but oil trains continued to Sinfin sidings.

Revival started at Shackerstone on 28th May 1978, when trains ran again to Market Bosworth. They were operated jointly by the latter's Light Railway and the former's Railway

Society. The terms Battlefield Steam Railway and, later, Battlefield Line were introduced, as the Bosworth Battlefield of 1485 is nearby. The extension south to Shenton took place on 2nd August 1992.

PASSENGER SERVICES

Many trains continued across at least two of the routes listed in the contents of this volume and so to tabulate them geographically would be complicated. Thus, we offer extracts from *Bradshaw Guides*, from the early and later days of the lines, to reveal the changes prior to their 1930s closures. The Sinfin service was soon reduced from hourly to peak hours only and ceased on 17th May 1993.

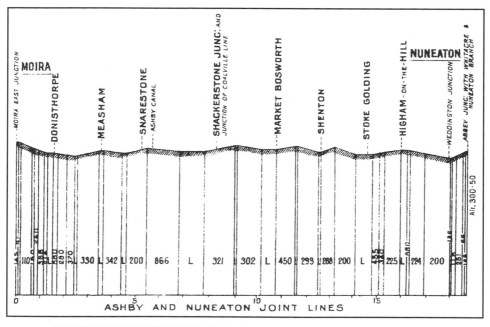

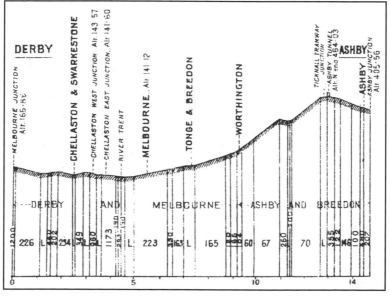

ASHBY and NUNEATON JOINT LINE.
London and North Western.

Fares frm Nuneaton. 1 cl.	2 cl.	gov	Euston Station,	mrn	mrn	aft	aft
			LONDON 128 ..dep	7 30	1010	3 0	5 10
			COVENTRY 137.. ,,	9 20	1145	4 50	6 45
s. d.	s. d.	s. d.	**Nuneaton (L. & N. W.)d**	1020	1 10	5 45	8 50
0 7	0 5	0 2½	Higham-on-the-Hill ..	1027	1 17	5 52	8 57
0 9	0 7	0 3½	Stoke Golding	1031	1 21	5 56	9 1
1 2	0 10	0 6	Shenton	1036	1 26	6 1	9 6
1 4	1 0	0 7½	**Market Bosworth**	1041	1 31	6 6	9 11
1 10	1 5	0 10	Shackerstone..........	1047	1 37	6 12	9 17
....	....	....	Shackerstone ....dep	1055	....	....	9 23
2 4	1 9	1 1	Heather	11 2	....	....	9 30
2 9	2 0	1 3	**Hugglescote** ....arr	11 7	....	....	9 35
2 4	1 9	1 1	Snareston	1055	1 45	6 20	9 25
2 9	2 0	1 3	Measham	11 0	1 50	6 26	9 30
3 0	2 3	1 4½	Donisthorpe	11 6	1 56	6 32	9 36
3 4	2 6	1 6½	Overseal and **Moira** arr	1111	2 1	6 37	9 41
From Market Bosworth.				mrn	mrn	aft	aft
			Overseal and Moira dp	8 10	1138	3 35	6 42
1 cl.	2 cl.	gov	Donisthorpe	8 14	1142	3 40	6 47
1 4	1 0	0 7	Measham..............	8 20	1149	3 46	6 53
1 0	0 9	0 5½	Snareston	8 25	1153	3 51	6 58
1 4	1 0	0 7	**Hugglescote** ....dep	8 10	....	....	6 45
1 0	0 9	0 5	Heather	8 15	....	....	6 50
....	....	....	Shackerstone ....arr	8 22	....	....	6 57
0 6	0 4	0 2	Shackerstone	8 33	12 0	3 58	7 5
....	....	....	**Market Bosworth**	8 40	12 4	4 5	7 12
0 4	0 3	0 1½	Shenton	8 44	12 8	4 10	7 17
0 8	0 6	0 3½	Stoke Golding	8 49	1213	4 15	7 22
1 0	0 9	0 5	Higham-on-the-Hill ..	8 53	1216	4 19	7 26
1 4	1 0	0 7½	**Nuneatn 137, 133, 128 a**	9 0	1223	4 26	7 33
3 0	2 3	1 5½	COVENTRY 137 arr	1010	1 15	5 44	9 20
15 4	12 0	8 8	**133** LONDON (Euston) ,,	1225	3 10	7 10	1040

June 1876

LOUGHBORO' and NUNEATON.—L. & N. W.

Euston Sta.,	gov	mrn	mrn	aft	gov	aft
LONDON 158 d	5 15	7 15	11 0	3 0	* Overseal and Moira Station.	6 30
179 COVENTRY ,,	6 50	9 5	1235	4 35		8 16
Nuneaton ..dep	7 40	9 50	1 37	5 45		9 5
Higham-on-Hill	7 47	9 57	1 44	5 52		9 12
Stoke Golding ..	7 51	10 1	1 48	5 56		9 16
Shenton	7 56	10 6	1 53	a		9 21
Mrkt Bosworth	8 1	1011	1 58	6 4		9 26
Shackerstone J.	8 7	1017	2 4	6 10		9 32
Shackerston J	....	1020	2 7	6 15	7 50	....
Snareston	....	1030	2 15	6 25	8 0	....
Measham	....	1034	2 19	6 29	8 4	....
Donisthorpe. .	....	1041	2 26	6 36	8 11	....
Overseal* arr	....	1047	2 32	6 42	8 17	....
Heather	8 14	1024	2 11	a	....	9 39
Hugglescote	8 19	1029	2 16	6 20	....	9 44
Coalville (East).	8 25	1035	2 22	6 25	....	9 50
Whitwick......	8 30	1040	2 27	6 30	....	9 55
Sheepshed [229	8 40	1050	2 37	6 40	....	10 5
Loughboro' arr	8 50	11 0	2 47	6 50	....	1015

Derby Road,	gov	mrn	mrn	aft	aft
Loughboro' dep	7 55	9 0	1115	3 25	7 0
Sheepshed......	8 5	9 10	1125	3 35	7 10
Whitwick......	8 15	9 20	1135	3 45	7 20
Coalville (East).	8 20	9 25	1140	3 50	7 25
Hugglescote....	8 26	9 31	1146	3 56	7 31
Heather	8 31	9 35	1151	4 1	7 36
Overseal* dep	8 5	....	1125	3 35	7 10
Donisthorpe. .	8 11	....	1131	3 38	7 16
Measham	8 18	....	1138	3 48	7 23
Snareston	8 22	....	1142	3 52	7 27
Shackerston J	8 32	....	1152	4 2	7 37
Shackerstone J.	8 38	9 43	1158	4 8	7 43
Mrkt Bosworth	8 44	9 49	12 4	4 14	7 49
Shenton........	8 49	9 54	12 9	4 19	7 54
Stoke Golding..	8 54	9 59	1214	4 24	7 59
Higham-on-Hill	8 58	10 3	1218	4 28	8 3
Nuneaton 179 a	9 5	1010	1225	4 35	8 10
COVENTRY 179	9 50	1130	1 20	5 30	9 25
163 LONDN (Eus)	1215	1 0	3 25	7 10	1120

a Stops on Sats.; and daily, when required, to set down from beyond Nuneaton.

February 1884

DERBY, ASHBY-DE-LA-ZOUCH, CASTLE DONINGTON, and TRENT.

Miles		Week Days.																	Sundays.			
		mrn	mrn	mrn	mrn	mrn		aft	aft	aft		aft	aft	aft	aft	aft			mrn		aft	aft
	Derby..................dep.	..	8 23	1022	10 33	1135	..	1 10	2 0	2 28	..	5 12	5 42	..	5 53	7 33	.	..	..	..	5 0	..
1½	Pear Tree and Normanton ..	....	8 28	1027	....	1140	....	1 15	2 5	2 35	....	5 17	5 47	....	5 58	7 38	....	....	....	....	....	....
4	Chellaston and Swarkestone.	..	8 37	1053	..	1147	..	1 21	2 13	2 42	..	5 23	5 53	..	6 3	7 44	.	..	..	..	5 10	6 12
7	Melbourne	....	....	1041	....	Sats. only.	....	1 29	....	2 52	....	5 30	....	....	6 12	7 52	....	....	....	....	5 20	....
8¾	Tonge and Breedon........	..	..	1046	..		..	1 35	..	2 59	..	Except Saturdays.	..	..	6 20	7 57	.	..	..	..	5 29	..
10¾	Worthington...[*below*, 687	....	....	1053	....		....	1 40	....	3 5	....		....	....	6 30	8 4	....	....	....	....	5 34	....
16¼	**Ashby-de-la-Zouch** arr.	..	..	11 6	..		..		..	3 21	..		..	..	6 42	8 16	.	..	..	..	..	..
6½	Weston-on-Trent ....[low	....	8 45	....	....	1154	....	Sats. only.	2 19	....	....		5 59	....	....	....	....	....	7 53	....	....	6 20
9¼	**Castle Donington & Shard-**	7 0	8 51	..	10 48	12 0	..		2 30	..	..		6 11	6 27	..	..	.	..	8 5	..	..	6 30
13½	**Trent 649, 695, 696** ..arr.	7 8	9 0	....	10 56	1210	....		2 40	....	....		....	6 39	....	....	....	....	8 16	....	....	6 40
22¾	**694** DERBY ....arr.	7 40	9 31	..	12 R 9	1230	..		3 17	..	..		..	7 27	..	..	.	..	1018	..	..	7 22
20½	**695** NOTTINGHAM .... ,,	7 35	9 27	....	11 16	1225	....		3 1	....	....		....	7 D 4	....	....	....	....	8 50	....	....	7 4

Miles.		Week Days.																	Sundays.			
		mrn	mrn	mrn	mrn	mrn	mrn	mrn		aft	aft	aft	aft		aft	aft	aft		aft			
	694 NOTTINGHAM ....dep.	6 18	..	7 18	Except Sats.	Sats. only.	9 5	..	..	1 14		..	5 15	..		..	7 26	..	..	..	..	..
	695 DERBY .... ,,	6 0	....	6 40			9 0	....	....	1218	Sats. only.	....	4 30	....		....	7 26	....	....	....	....	....
6¾	**Trent**..................dep.	6 42	..	7 39			9 28	..	..	1 32		..	5 39	..	Except Saturdays.	..	7 54	..	To Trent.	..	..	..
11	**Castle Donington & Shard-**	6 50	....	7 50			9 37	....	....	1 43		....	5 48	....		....	8 5	....		....	....	....
13¾	Weston-on-Trent.........[low	..	..	7 57			9 44	..	..	1 48		..	5 53	..		..	8 13	..		..	..	..
—	Mls **Ashby-de-la-Zouch** .dep.	....	....	....	7 55	8 0	....	1115	....	Sats. only.		3 55	....	....		7 15	....	....	....	....	....	....
—	5¼ Worthington	..	..	..	8 10	8 15	..	1128	..		1 45	4 9	..	..		7 28	..	..	5 43	..	..	..
—	7¾ Tonge and Breedon	....	....	....	8 15	8 20	....	1133	....		1 50	4 15	....	....		7 33	....	....	5 49	....	....	....
—	9¼ Melbourne	..	6 56	..	8 22	8 27	..	1138	..		1 55	4 23	..	..	6 2	7 38	..	..	5 55	..	..	..
16¼	Chellaston and Swarkestone.	....	7 3	8 8	8 30	8 35	9 52	1145	....	1 55	2 3	4 33	6 3	....	6 10	7 48	8 22	....	6 7	....	....	....
18¾	Pear Tree and Normanton...	..	7 10	8 15	..	..	..	..	..	2 3	2 12	4 42	6 12	..	6 18	7 57	8 30	..	..	..	..	..
20¼	**Derby A 642, 656, 664.** arr.	....	7 15	8 20	8 40	8 45	10 3	1155	....	2 7	2 17	4 48	6 17	....	6 23	8 2	8 34	....	....	....	....	....

A Over 1 mile to Friargate Station. D Arrives at 6 57 aft. on Saturdays.
R Arrives at 11 29 mrn. on Mondays and Fridays, and at 12 5 aft. on Saturdays.

July 1929

Saturday service will apply on Bank Holidays 29 May, 28 August, 1 January, 16 April and 7 May

Mondays to Fridays

Sinfin, Derby and Matlock

Second Class only

Miles																								
0	**Sinfin Central**	d	..	..	07 20	..	08 11	..	..	..	..	..	..	16 05	..	16 48	..	..	..	..	..	..	..	..
¼	Sinfin North	d	..	..	..	..	08 13	..	..	..	..	..	..	16 07	..	16 50	..	..	..	..	..	..	..	..
1½	Peartree	d	..	..	..	..	08 15	..	..	..	..	..	..	16 09	..	16 52	..	..	..	..	..	..	..	..
2½	**Derby**	a	..	..	07 25	..	08 19	..	..	..	..	..	..	16 13	..	16 56	..	..	..	..	..	..	..	..
—	**53** London St. Pancras	d	..	..	..	..	*04 25*	..	*07 50*	*08 46*	..	*10 53*	..	*13 53*	..	*14 04*	..	..	..	*15 55*	..	*18 15*	*19 14*	..
—	**80** Nottingham	d	..	..	*06 39*	..	*07 30*	..	*09 39*	*10 34*	..	*13 39*	..	*15 39*	..	*16 10*	..	*16 39*	..	*17 39*	..	*19 34*	*21 39*	..
0	**Derby**	d	07 08	..	07 26	..	08 21	..	10 15	12 05	..	14 17	..	16 15	..	16 57	..	17 40	..	18 20	..	20 28	22 15	..
5¼	Duffield	d	07 16	..	07 34	..	08 29	..	10 23	12 13	..	14 25	..	16 23	..	17 05	..	17 48	..	18 28	..	20 36	22 23	..
7¾	Belper	d	07 21	..	07 39	..	08 34	..	10 28	12 18	..	14 30	..	16 28	..	17 10	..	17 53	..	18 33	..	20 41	22 28	..
10¼	Ambergate	d	07a27	..	07 46	..	08 40	..	10 34	12 24	..	14 36	..	16 34	..	17 17	..	17 59	..	18 39	..	20 47	22 34	..
12½	Whatstandwell	d	..	..	..	..	08 45	..	10 39	12 29	..	14 41	..	16 39	..	17 21	..	18 04	..	18 44	..	20 52	22 39	..
15½	Cromford	d	..	..	..	..	08 50	..	10 44	12 34	..	14 46	..	16 44	..	17 27	..	18 09	..	18 49	..	20 57	22 44	..
16¼	Matlock Bath	d	..	..	..	..	08 53	..	10 47	12 37	..	14 49	..	16 47	..	17 29	..	18 12	..	18 52	..	21 00	22 47	..
17¼	**Matlock**	a	..	..	07 56	..	08 56	..	10 50	12 40	..	14 52	..	16 50	..	17 33	..	18 15	..	18 55	..	21 03	22 50	..

Will also apply Bank Holiday Mondays 29 May, 28 August, 1 January, 16 April and 7 May

Saturdays

Second Class only

Sinfin Central	d	..	..	..	..	..	..	..	..	..	..	..	..	..	..	..	..	..	..	..	..	..	..	..
Sinfin North	d	..	..	..	..	..	..	..	..	..	..	..	..	..	..	..	..	..	..	..	..	..	..	..
Peartree	d	..	..	..	..	..	..	..	..	..	..	..	..	..	..	..	..	..	..	..	..	..	..	..
Derby	a	..	..	..	..	..	..	..	..	..	..	..	..	..	..	..	..	..	..	..	..	..	..	..
53 London St. Pancras	d	..	..	*04 25*	..	*07 50*	..	*11 01*	..	..	*13 01*	..	..	..	..	*15 01*	..	..	..	*17 01*	..	*19 01*	..	..
80 Nottingham	d	*06 48*	..	*07 30*	..	*09 39*	..	*12 39*	..	..	*14 39*	..	..	*15 39*	..	*16 39*	..	*17 15*	..	*17 39*	..	*20 42*	..	..
Derby	d	07 26	..	08 21	..	10 15	..	13 17	..	..	15 17	..	..	16 15	..	17 23	..	18 02	..	19 08	..	21 22	..	..
Duffield	d	07 34	..	08 29	..	10 23	..	13 25	..	..	15 25	..	..	16 23	..	17 31	..	18 10	..	19 16	..	21 30	..	..
Belper	d	07 39	..	08 34	..	10 28	..	13 30	..	..	15 30	..	..	16 28	..	17 36	..	18 15	..	19 21	..	21 35	..	..
Ambergate	d	07 46	..	08 40	..	10 34	..	13 36	..	..	15 36	..	..	16 34	..	17 42	..	18 21	..	19 27	..	21 41	..	..
Whatstandwell	d	..	..	08 45	..	10 39	..	13 41	..	..	15 41	..	..	16 39	..	17 47	..	18 26	..	19 32	..	21 46	..	..
Cromford	d	..	..	08 50	..	10 44	..	13 46	..	..	15 46	..	..	16 44	..	17 52	..	18 31	..	19 37	..	21 51	..	..
Matlock Bath	d	..	..	08 53	..	10 47	..	13 49	..	..	15 49	..	..	16 47	..	17 55	..	18 34	..	19 40	..	21 54	..	..
Matlock	a	07 56	..	08 56	..	10 50	..	13 52	..	..	15 52	..	..	16 50	..	17 58	..	18 37	..	19 43	..	21 57	..	..

No Sunday service

May 1978

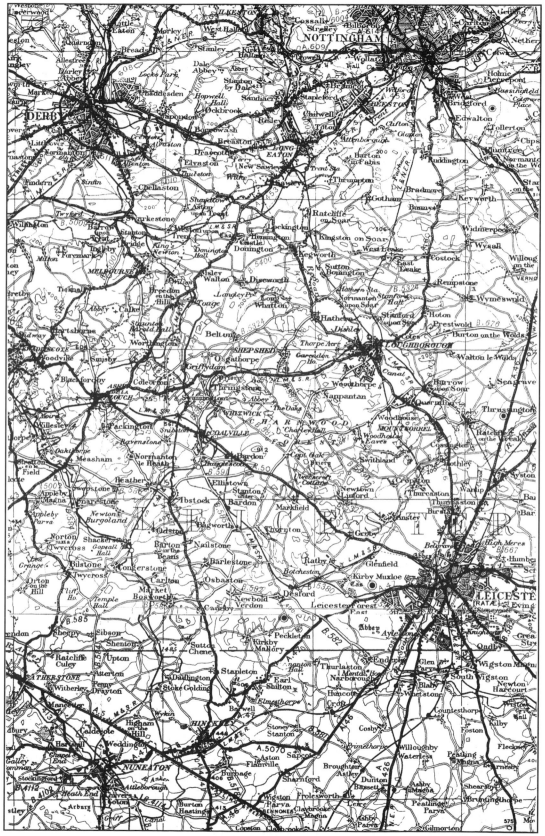

Ib. The 1946 revision is at 1ins to 1 mile.

1. Nuneaton to Hugglescote

NUNEATON ABBEY STREET

From its early days, the line was an alternative route for express goods traffic between the north of England and London. These trains passed along the branch at night and, in addition, express milk trains, from the pasture lands of Derbyshire to Euston, used it for many years, while a newspaper train from Manchester to Euston also appeared. The primary object of the line was to afford facilities for southbound coal traffic from the mining areas of North Leicestershire. About 10 mineral trains reached Nuneaton daily from the Moira and Coalville districts. In July 1890, the number was nearly doubled, when a through passenger service from Burton to Nuneaton was inaugurated, which also gave connection with the North Staffordshire lines to Ashbourne and other places. By 1892, this service had been extended to provide through trains to Manchester, via Leek and Macclesfield.

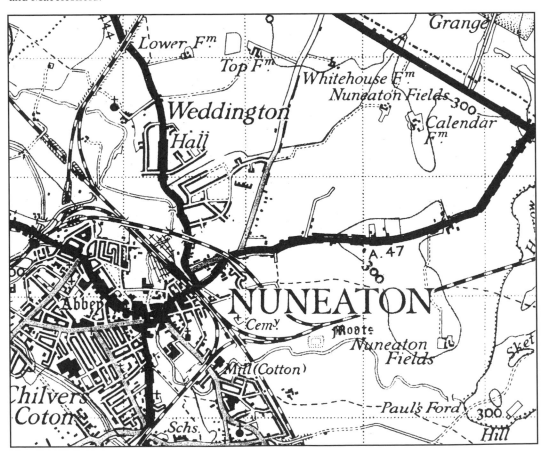

II. The 1946 edition at 2ins to 1 mile has the junctions at their maximum. Abbey Street station is circular and is on the left, on the Birmingham line of 1864. Clockwise are: the Tamworth route (1847), the Ashby line (1873), the Hinckley route (1862), the Rugby line (1847) and the Coventry route (1850). Trent Valley station is rectangular and is towards the centre. Weddington Junction is to the left of its church. Its signal box had 16 levers and closed on 18th July 1971. South of it is Ashby Junction; the curve closed on 17th August 1969.

III. The line from Birmingham is lower left on this 1914 survey and our route to Coalville is at the upper border. The connections to the Trent Valley station are top right. The lines top left served the quarries; the loop has a dock, which can be seen in picture 5.

London & North Western Ry.
Issued subject to the conditions & regulations in the Cos Time Tables Books Bills & Notices & unless stated therein to be so NOT available by Irish Mail.
LOUGHBORO' TO
NUNEATON (L.&N.W.)
THIRD CLASS] ·315(S.) [Parly
NUNEATON FARE 2/2½
06 SE14
3065

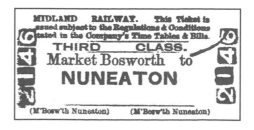

MIDLAND RAILWAY. This Ticket is issued subject to the Regulations & Conditions stated in the Company's Time Tables & Bills.
THIRD CLASS.
Market Bosworth to
NUNEATON
(M'Bosw'th Nuneaton) (M'Bosw'th Nuneaton)
7146
2049

1.	This 1935 panorama is eastwards and has Abbey Junction Box beyond the bridge arch, which carried Midland Road. The first station had been ¼ mile to the west and was in use until 1st September 1873. (J.Alsop coll.)

2.	We gain the prospective passenger's perspective on 21st July 1951 and see just pre-war road transport. With such a fine frontage, one would not expect to find the platforms devoid of roofing. The goods yard closed on 2nd October 1972; it had a 10-ton crane. (J.Alsop coll.)

For other views of this station, see our *Birmingham to Tamworth & Nuneaton* **album. Trent Valley station is included in the latter, and is also in** *Rugby to Stafford* **and** *Coventry to Leicester*.

3.   Seen in about 1968, a DMU is signalled for the line to Hinckley. Such units were introduced on the Birmingham-Leicester route in March 1958. The station closed on 4th March 1968. (SLS coll.)

4.   The Ashby & Nuneaton line, which closed as far as Measham Colliery in 1971, goes off to the left. To the left of the signalbox is the Midland Loop of 1880 leading to the west side of Nuneaton Trent Valley. To the right of the box is the original Midland line of 1864, which crossed the LNW main line and joined the LNW's South Leicestershire line towards Leicester at Midland Junction, and which closed on 15th February 1992. All of this is shown on map XXVI in *Birmingham to Tamworth & Nuneaton*. The route of the original line was re-opened from 7th June 2004 from here across the LNW main line. From there it was diverted to serve two new platforms, nos 6 & 7, on the east side of Nuneaton Trent Valley. The box had 55 levers and was in use from 1925 to 1992. (R.Humm coll.)

5.   We look more closely at the signal on the left of the previous picture. On the left is the private siding of Judkins Stone Quarries. Waiting at the signal on 9th October 1954 is class 5MT 2-6-0 no. 42852, piloting class 4F 0-6-0 no. 44138. The coal train is from Coalville. (R.S.Carpenter coll.)

HIGHAM-ON-THE-HILL

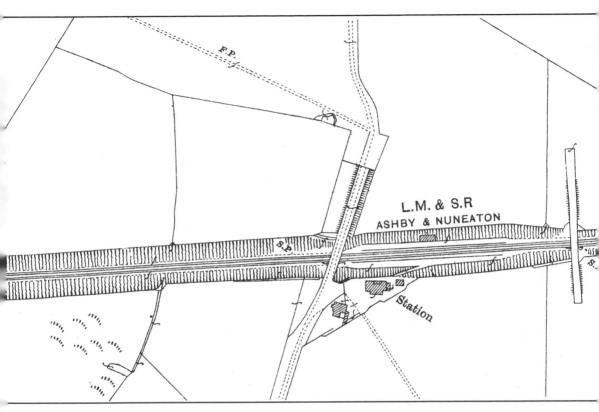

IV. The platforms are in a cutting and the main building is at the top of an inclined path from the up one. The station opened with the line, on 1st September 1873. Its relationship to the village is shown on the next map.

6.   This poor quality picture appears to be the only one taken here and is of the down side, looking north. Closure came on 12th April 1931 and the platforms were removed in 1936. All traffic ceased on the line in 1971 and the route became the Weddington Country Walk. (A.Dudman coll.)

STOKE GOLDING

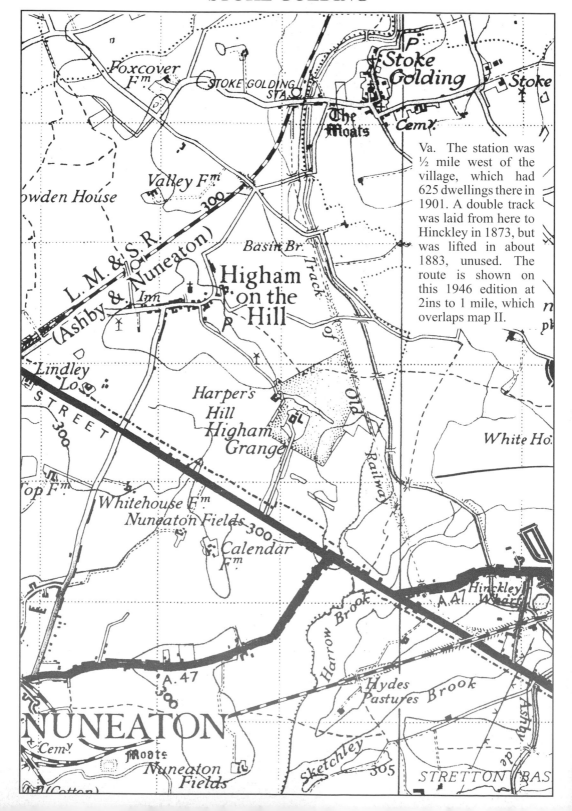

Va. The station was ½ mile west of the village, which had 625 dwellings there in 1901. A double track was laid from here to Hinckley in 1873, but was lifted in about 1883, unused. The route is shown on this 1946 edition at 2ins to 1 mile, which overlaps map II.

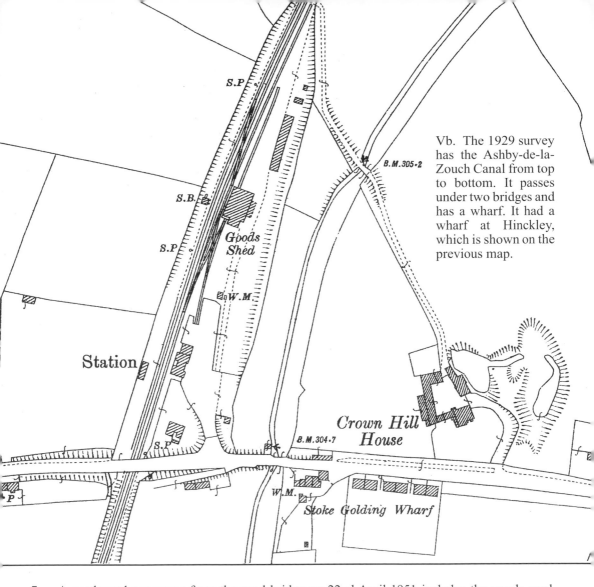

S.P.

B.M.305·2

Vb. The 1929 survey has the Ashby-de-la-Zouch Canal from top to bottom. It passes under two bridges and has a wharf. It had a wharf at Hinckley, which is shown on the previous map.

S.B.

S.P.

Goods Shed

W.M.

Station

Crown Hill House

S.P.

B.M.304·7

P

W.M.

Stoke Golding Wharf

7.   A northward panorama from the road bridge on 22nd April 1951 includes the goods yard, which closed on 6th August 1962. There was a 30-cwt crane listed here, but it was inside the goods shed. The signal box was in use from 1872 until 7th August 1962. (J.Alsop coll.)

8.   The last passenger left in April 1931 and this is the sad scene on 22nd May 1965. Freight trains continued to run through until 1971 and, later, the premises became dwellings. The goods yard was developed as an industrial estate. (R.M.Casserley)

9.   Running south on 30th October 1965 is no. D7555 with a coal train. The goods shed was retained for commercial purposes. Parcel traffic had continued here until 2nd July 1951. The house for the station master was to the right of the camera. It remains standing as a residence. (M.J.Stretton coll.)

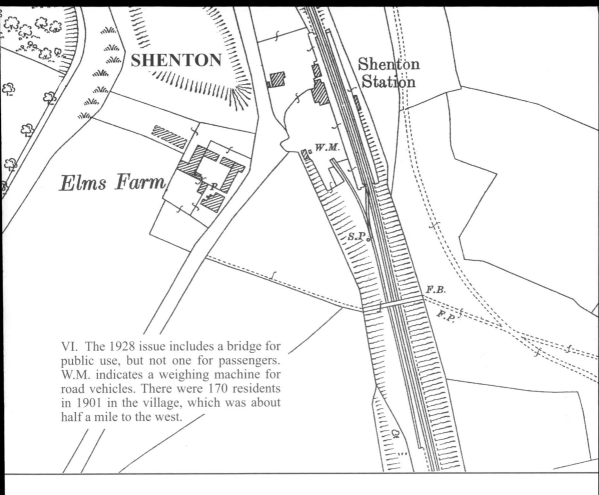

SHENTON

Shenton
Station

Elms Farm

W.M.

S.P.

F.B.

F.P.

VI. The 1928 issue includes a bridge for public use, but not one for passengers. W.M. indicates a weighing machine for road vehicles. There were 170 residents in 1901 in the village, which was about half a mile to the west.

10.   On the left is the weighing office and a van stands at the short side dock, which also has an end dock. Beyond it is the spacious accommodation for the station master. Closure was thus: passengers 13th April 1931, parcels 2nd July 1951 and goods 4th June 1956. Only the house and the lamp hut were to remain, long term. (P.Laming coll.)

11. The station was situated midway between the small villages of Sutton Cheney and Shenton. For several years, prior to 1920, it had less than 10 bookings per week. The excursion trains around 1960 had not called here. Southbound in mist on 13th September 1965, is no. 48359, a class 8F 2-8-0, hauling coal. (M.J.Stretton coll.)

12. The location became the southern terminus of the Battlefield Steam Railway on 2nd August 1992. This building had stood at Leicester Humberstone Road and was rebuilt here in 1993. The photograph was taken on 18th April 2009, with DMU no. 51131 on duty. (P.Barnes)

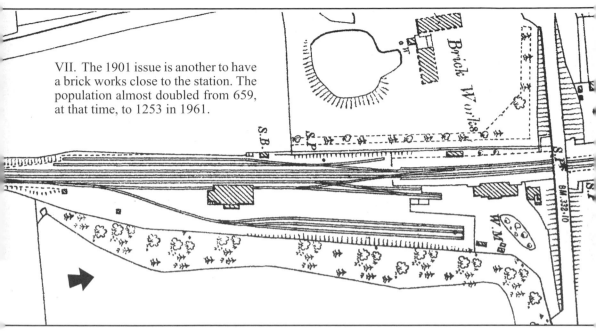

VII. The 1901 issue is another to have a brick works close to the station. The population almost doubled from 659, at that time, to 1253 in 1961.

13. MR 2-2-2 no. 35 was one of a series of 20 built at Derby between 1863 and 1866. It is still in the original Midland green livery and is not fitted with continuous brakes. The coaches are four wheelers with oil lighting. An LNW class DX 0-6-0 is on the other road facing Nuneaton, in this 1883 view. (LOSA)

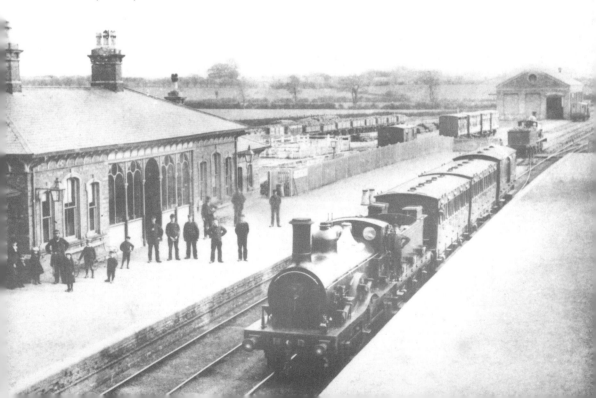

14.   The eastern facade was recorded in around 1900. Passenger service ceased on 13th April 1931, but occasional excursion trains called from the mid-1950s until 1962. It was later used by Station Garage. (LOSA)

15.   After closure to passengers, the main building was used by goods staff, until taken over by the Army in 1939. It extended the yard for petrol distribution purposes and added narrow gauge tracks. The panorama is from 5th September 1957. (Milepost 92½)

16. Determined to retain a link with steam following its rapid decline on BR, local enthusiasts arranged a gathering of road engines in the station approach on 10th April 1964. A nearby water main had to be accessed, using the same method as the fire brigade; via a yellow sign bearing a black H. (J.Alsop coll.)

17. This view from 13th September 1965 includes the Army's kitchen extension and the 16-lever signal box of LNWR origin. Its closure came on 18th July 1971. Class 8F 2-8-0 no. 48471 blows off as nos D5259 and D7548 await to use the single line north. (M.J.Stretton coll.)

18.   The station was reopened on 26th March 1978. Bearing the initials of the Market Bosworth Light Railway, Hawthorn Leslie 0-6-0ST no. 3931 of 1938 waits on 8th August 1982. It has run round and returned to Shackerstone. (T.Heavyside)

19.   The 1987 ticket office and shop are seen on 19th August 2013. On the right is the waiting room, which had been at Chester Road, Birmingham, and was reconstructed here by local supporters. (M.Turvey)

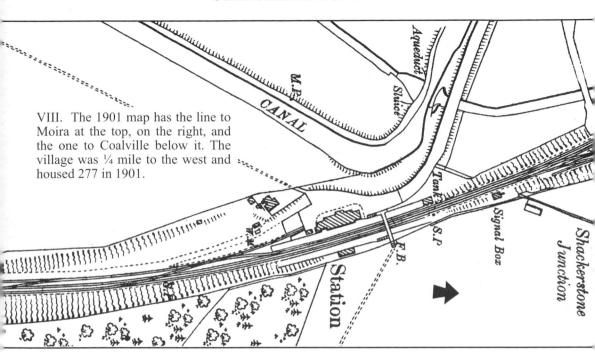

VIII. The 1901 map has the line to Moira at the top, on the right, and the one to Coalville below it. The village was ¼ mile to the west and housed 277 in 1901.

20. The funeral cortège of Countess Howe is included as many details are of interest and the family was involved in the creation of the railway. (P.Laming coll.)

22. The west elevation was still in good order on 14th April 1957, although passenger closure had taken place on 13th April 1931. Just visible is Junction Box and a Morris Minor. (R.M.Casserley)

21.   A panorama from 1st August 1954, northwards, includes Junction Box and just one sign. It was for the benefit of gentlemen only. The box opened on 24th June 1890 and was in use until 29th November 1964. (R.Humm coll.)

23.   The LCGB Burton Area Tour is seen on 1st March 1959, being propelled by no. 41328, a class 2 2-6-2T. It started at Derby Midland and ran via Woodville, Moira, Ashby, Coalville and then Gresley, Burton and Eggington. Return was at 5.28pm. (E.Wilmshurst)

24. No. D7534 is northbound on the remaining single track with mixed freight on 11th September 1967. The goods yard here had closed on 2nd March 1964. Still standing was the weigh house office, with its single chimney. (M.J.Stretton coll.)

ASHBY and NUNEATON.—Midland.

Mls frm Ashby.	Fares 1 cl.	3 cl.	Station Street,	mrn	mrn	mrn	aft
			Burton..........dep	7 40	....	11 5	5 43
	0 8	0 5	Gresley.......... ,,	7 50	....	1115	5 53
	1 4	0 9¼	**Ashby**........ ,,	7 53	....	1135	6 5
2¼	1 1	0 7	Moira...............	8 1	....	1142	6 12
4¼	1 4	0 8¼	Donisthorpe.........	8 6	....	1148	6 17
6	1 7	0 10	Measham	8 10	....	1155	6 23
7¾	1 11	1 0	Snarestone	8 15	....	noon	6 29
—	....	....	186 London (St. Pan) d	....	5 15	12 0	....
—	1 1	2 6½	Leicester*... ,,	....	9 10	2 30	....
—	2 0	1 2½	— Coalville ....dep	7 50	1010	3 35	....
—	2 5	1 3½	2 Hugglescote .. ,,	7 58	1018	3 43	....
—	2 5	1 3½	4 Heather...... ,,	8 7	1032	3 57	....
—	....	....	6¾ Shackerstone arr	8 15	1040	4 7	....
10¾	2 4	1 3½	Shackerstone......	8 22	1044	4 12	6 37
13¼	2 7	1 5	Market Bosworth...	8 28	1050	4 18	6 43
15	2 10	1 7	Shenton............	8 33	Campbell Street.*	....	6 48
17	3 1	1 9½	Stoke Golding......	8 39		....	6 54
18¼	3 3	1 10½	Higham........[204	8 44		....	6 59
21	3 9	2 1½	**Nuneaton** (Mid.) ar	8 50		....	7 5
41½	....	....	204 Birmingham ar	9 55		....	7 55
84½	....	....	Bristol 199	2 10		....	1115

Temple Street Sta.,	mrn	mrn	aft	aft
Bristol 200 dep	....	....	....	3 20
204 Birmingham ,,	7 40	....	....	6 45
Nuneaton (Mid.) dep	9 5	....	....	7 30
Higham..............	9 11	....	....	7 37
Stoke Golding......	9 16	....	....	7 43
Shenton............	9 22	....	....	7 49
Market Bosworth...	9 27	11 0	5 20	7 54
Shackerstone......	9 33	11 6	5 26	7 59
Shackerstone dep	9 37	11 8	5 29	...
Heather...........	9 44	1114	5 35	...
Hugglescote	9 52	1121	5 45	....
Coalville, *see abvea*	10 0	1133	6 0	....
Leicester* arr	....	1222	7 5	....
189 London (St. Pan) ,,	....	2 55	9 50	....
Snarestone..........	9 40	aft	....	8 7
Measham	9 45	2 40	....	8 12
Donisthorpe........	9 50	2 46	....	8 17
Moira..............	9 56	2 53	....	8 23
Ashby 197 ....arr	10 2	3 0	....	8 30
Gresley ....[108 ,,	1018	3 37	....	8 36
Burton 201, 198, 183	1025	3 50	....	8 45

June 1876

25.   In the distance, on 13th August 1978, is a signal box just moved from Measham. It had previously been at Worthington and housed a lever frame from Uttoxeter. It came into use here in 1978. Arriving is Bagnall 0-6-0ST no. 3059 of 1954. (T.Heavyside)

26.   Seen on the same day is the other end of the same engine, with the unusual Giesl ejector on its smokebox. It had formerly worked hauling North Staffordshire coal at Florence Colliery. (T.Heavyside)

27.   A final picture from the same day features Hawthorn Leslie 0-6-0ST no. 3931 of 1938, with crowds of admirers. It carries on its saddle tank the initials MBLR: the Market Bosworth Light Railway. The museum had been established in the building on the left. (T.Heavyside)

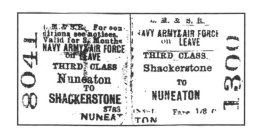

28. We can now enjoy a photo from 14th August 2004. This shows the north end of the system, where sidings have been laid on the site of Shackerstone Junction. No. D5518 runs round the 16.00 to Shenton, which waits behind the cameraman, who is on the footbridge. (P.Barnes)

29. It is important to include the engine shed, as it is the site of a vast range of essential repair work. Austerity 0-6-0ST *Cumbria* is passing it during the Santa Train service on 10th December 2016. This was one of the smaller locomotives, while the railway was expanding its range to include ex-BR locomotives. (Shackerstone Railway Society)

CADEBY LIGHT RAILWAY

30.   The Reverend Teddy Boston purchased a retired 2ft gauge quarry locomotive in 1962 and ran it on a 97yd long track in the garden of his rectory at Cadeby, which is about one mile east of Market Bosworth. He is at the controls of *Pixie* on 12th August 1978. It was Bagnall 0-4-0ST no. 2090 of 1919. Sadly, the vicar died in 1986, but his widow kept the line operating. (T.Heavyside)

➔   31. *Pixie* is seen running on the same day with the owner's church in the background. The line ran on selected days from 1963 until 2005. By 2003, there were 19 other 2ft gauge locomotives on site, all internal combustion, plus two road steam engines. The model railway was one of the biggest ever built. Teddy showed the joys of the faith and rail pleasures together. The railway closed in 2006 and most of the collection moved to the Apedale Railway. (T.Heavyside)

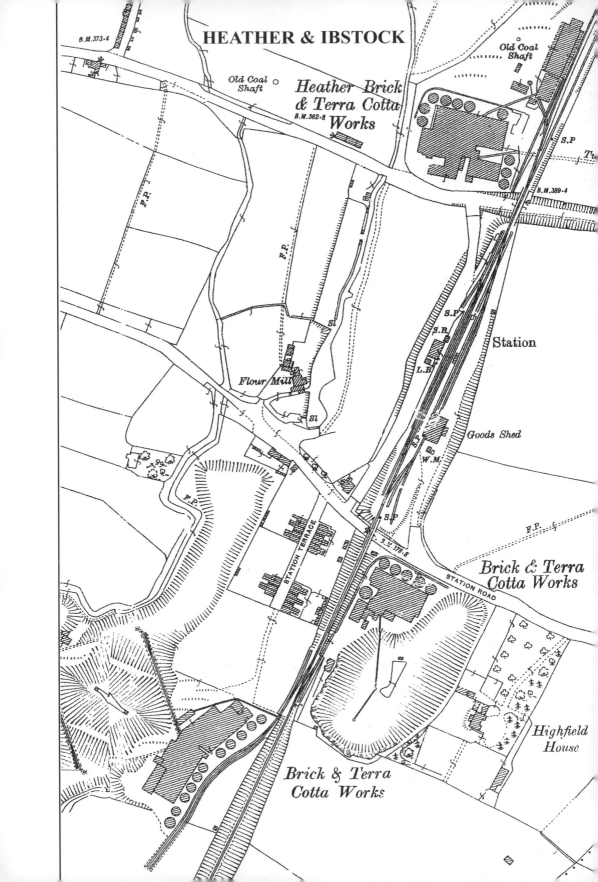

HEATHER & IBSTOCK

B.M.373.4

Old Coal
Shaft

Old Coal
Shaft

Heather Brick
& Terra Cotta
Works

B.M.362.8

S.P

B.M.389.4

Station

Flour Mill

S.P
S.B
L.B

Goods Shed

S.P
W.M.

S.P

F.P.

Brick & Terra
Cotta Works

STATION TERRACE

STATION ROAD

B.M.378.8

Highfield
House

Brick & Terra
Cotta Works

← IX. The 1929 edition is shown at 20ins to 1 mile and has a colliery site, top right. The circles represent kilns. The station opened with the line on 1st September 1873.

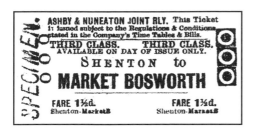

32. A postcard from around 1900 gives a comprehensive coverage of the architectural details. Heather had 624 folk housed in 1901, while Ibstock had 3922. This had risen to 4954 by 1961. (J.Alsop coll.)

33.   Passenger service ceased on 13th April 1931 and we examine the station on 30th August 1956. The brickworks' chimneys appear in all the views. This one is northwards. (R.Humm coll.)

34.   The suffix & IBSTOCK was added on 1st September 1894. We look south on 27th May 1957 and see the goods shed, which housed a 25cwt crane. The yard closed on 7th June 1954. The signal box opened in 1933; there had been two previously: Colliery North and Colliery South. (R.Humm coll.)

HUGGLESCOTE

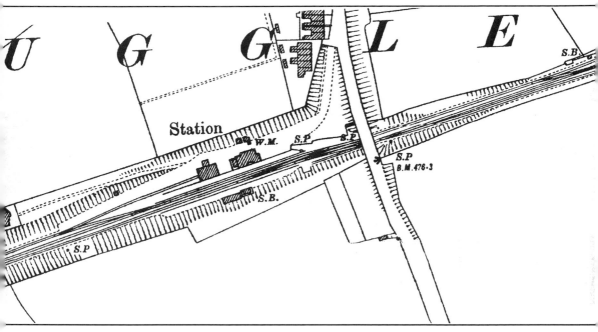

X. The 1927 survey includes a waiting room adjacent to the signal box, but only the latter appears in the photographs. Passenger service had ended on 13th April 1931. The village is shown on the next map.

35. This westward view is from 22nd April 1951 and it includes the goods office and weigh house on the right. The wagons had to be horse drawn or man handled to the goods shed. (R.Humm coll.)

36. Passing through is class 4F 0-6-0 no. 44437. This was the second signal box here, which opened on 11th March 1894 and closed on 4th July 1965. The photo is from 12th April 1958, as is the next one. (M.J.Stretton coll.)

37. Parcel traffic ceased on 2nd July 1951 and goods followed on 6th April 1964. The hut near the road bridge was for the track gang. The platform edge has collapsed opposite the signal box. East of the station had been a siding for the South Leicestershire Colliery & Brick Company. It is shown on the next map. It opened in 1879 and closed in 1891. (M.J.Stretton coll.)

38.   Charnwood Forest Junction is close to the 'gg' of Hugglescote on the next map. We are looking back towards Nuneaton from a SLS tour train on 3rd May 1952. The 1908 signal box had 28 levers and closed on 4th July 1965. At the north end of it was Coalville Junction. Coalville Town and its nearby lines appear in our *Leicester to Burton* album. (R.S.Carpenter coll.)

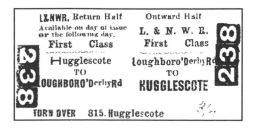

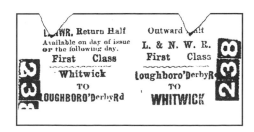

2. Coalville to Loughborough

COALVILLE EAST

Charnwood Forest Railway

XI. Seen at 2ins to 1 mile is this 1946 edition. Its thick curly line is the 500ft contour. The single line from Nuneaton is lower left, together with the closed Hugglescote station. It passes under the double track of the Leicester to Burton line and also has a connection to it. See our album of that name, to find Coalville Town station.

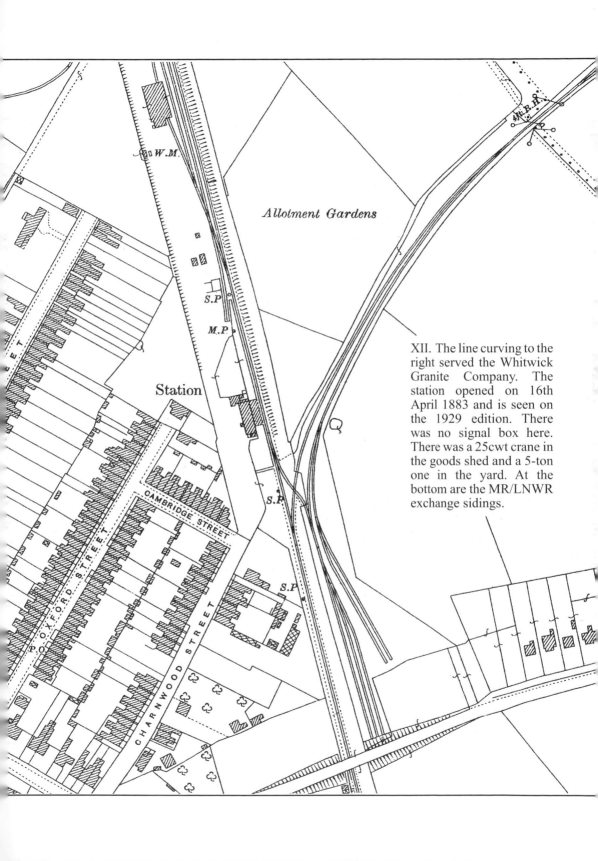

W.M.

Allotment Gardens

4*.P.H.

S.P

M.P

Station

CAMBRIDGE STREET

OXFORD STREET

CHARNWOOD STREET

P.O

S.P

S.P

S.P

XII. The line curving to the right served the Whitwick Granite Company. The station opened on 16th April 1883 and is seen on the 1929 edition. There was no signal box here. There was a 25cwt crane in the goods shed and a 5-ton one in the yard. At the bottom are the MR/LNWR exchange sidings.

39. Although closed to passengers on 13th April 1931, all was in good order on 10th October 1935. There was an eight-lever signal frame controlling the signals in the distance. (W.A.Camwell/SLS)

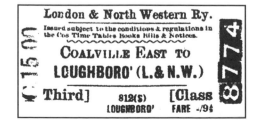

London & North Western Ry.

Issued subject to the conditions & regulations in the Cos Time Tables Books Bills & Notices.

COALVILLE EAST TO

LOUGHBORO' (L.& N.W.)

Third] 812(S) [Class
LOUGHBORO' FARE -/9½

8774

London & North Western Ry.

Issued subject to the conditions & regulations in the Cos Time Tables Books Bills & Notices

SHEPSHED TO

LOUGHBORO' (L.& N.W.)
(P)

Third] 814(S) [Class
LOUGHBORO' FARE -/3½

3260

40.   Seen on the same day is ex-MR class 2F 0-6-0 no. 3642. There were still 327 in use in 1944. The crossing gave foot access to the gates across the two private sidings. Coalville had 14 in total. The yard closed on 7th October 1963. (W.A.Camwell/SLS)

41.   The exterior is pictured on 12th May 1962, along with the photographer's widely illustrated 1935 Morris 12. The suffix East was used until 1st May 1905 and, again, from 2nd June 1924. LNW was used in the interim. (R.M.Casserley)

WHITWICK

Duke of Newcastle
(P.H.)

Club

Methodist Chapel
(Wesleyan)

G. Yd.

St. John
the Baptist's Church
(Vicarage)

Baptist Church

XIII. The 1923 edition reveals the proximity of the station to the town centre and Market Place. Cattle were conveyed by rail until the early 1960s and the fencing below the word BRANCH suggests cattle pens. Goods yard closure was on 7th October 1963.

Elastic Web Manufactory

Inn

Grave Yard

Station

Castle
(Site of

Castle Hill

Railway Hotel

Bk.
P.O.
Bank

all Ground

Schools

odge

Club

ETERY

W.M.

Picture Theatre

L. & N. W. R.
CHARNWOOD FOREST BRANCH

Goods Shed

King's Arms
(P.H.)

Recreation Ground

42.   The town had 3720 residents in 1901 and this postcard was produced about that time. The right of the cutting had been dug into the side of a hill that had earlier supported an important castle. (LOSA)

43.   The route from Coalville to here became a public footpath, but the stairs were removed in the 1990s. The building was eventually occupied by the Whitwick Historical Group and was painted Midland Railway red. It is seen on 28th August 1960. The church in the background acquired its tower in 1910. (M.J.Stretton coll.)

44. The booking hall was at street level, at the top of the steps. Seen in 1962, the building had been leased out as a shop for many years, although previously it had been used by a blacksmith. (R.M.Casserley)

45. The Railway Enthusiasts Club travelled the line on 14th April 1957. Nearest is a BR Mk I coach bearing the roof board 'The Charnwood Forester'. It ran from King's Cross via Holme, Ramsey North, Market Harborough, Desford and reversed at Shepshed. The five coaches returned to King's Cross via Shenton, both Nuneaton stations, Wigston, Kettering and Hitchin. (M.J.Stretton coll.)

NORTH OF WHITWICK

Thringstone

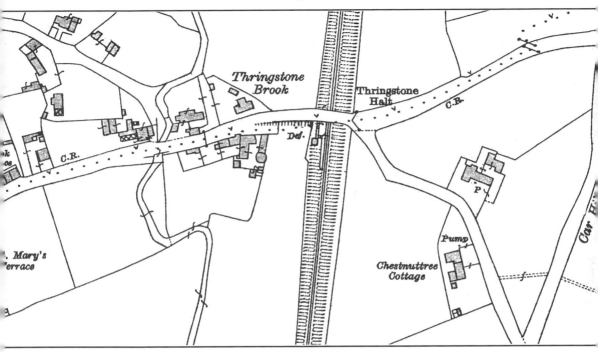

XIV. No pictures have been found of the branch halts. All three were open from 2nd April 1907 to 13th April 1931. Seen at the bottom of the steps is a hut, which was added in 1914. Each platform had two oil lamps that were tended by the guard. The platforms were 60ft long and made of old sleepers.

Grace Dieu Halt

XV. Another 1927 extract and this includes some transport history; the Charnwood Forest Canal. This halt had some extra Summer traffic, as there were visitors to the ruins of the Priory after which it was named. The hut arrived in 1911. An impressive six-arch viaduct still stands. This once carried the branch south of the halt.

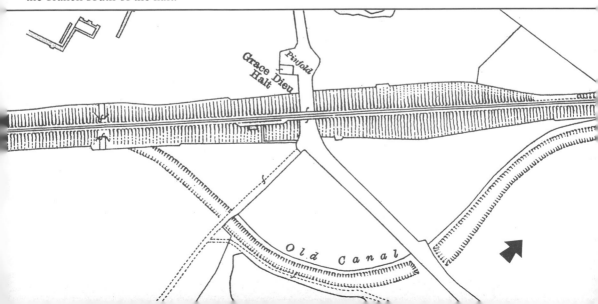

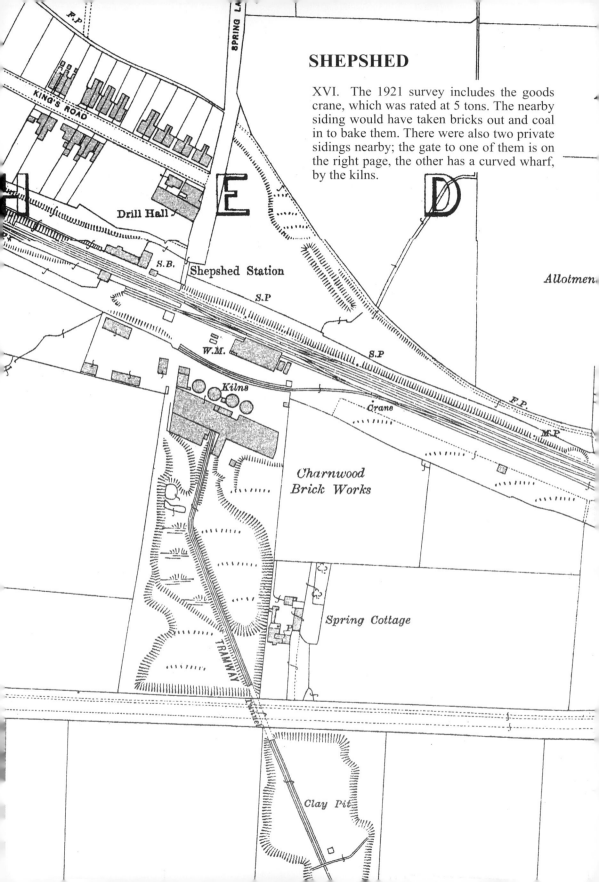

SHEPSHED

XVI. The 1921 survey includes the goods crane, which was rated at 5 tons. The nearby siding would have taken bricks out and coal in to bake them. There were also two private sidings nearby; the gate to one of them is on the right page, the other has a curved wharf, by the kilns.

King's Road

F.P.

SPRING LANE

Drill Hall

S.B.

Shepshed Station

S.P.

S.P.

W.M.

Kilns

Crane

F.P.

M.P.

Charnwood Brick Works

Allotmen.

Spring Cottage

TRAMWAY

Clay Pit

46. The up platform is on the right and serves the passing loop. The town had a population of 5293 in 1901 and its centre was about ½ mile to the north of the station. (P.Laming coll.)

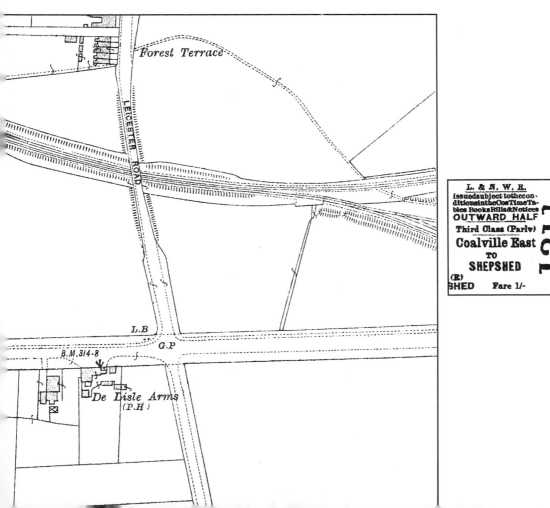

47. The station gardens won awards for many years. Sadly, only one of the beds is visible. The name used until May 1888 was SHEEPSHED. Lower right is the rodding tunnel, which ran to the signal box. (J.Alsop coll.)

48. The route was known as the 'Bluebell Line' by passengers at one period. Crews later termed it the 'Bread & Herring Line', probably because it was a popular snack on the job. The card's postmark was 1911. (P.Laming coll.)

49. Seen on 27th May 1961 is the Leicestershire Railway Society's railtour, which had started from Leicester London Road at 2.15pm. No. 41321 was a class 2MT 2-6-2T of recent construction. (E.Wilmshurst)

50.   After the closure to passengers on 13th April 1931, part of the building was used as a goods office. Goods traffic ended on 7th October 1963 and complete closure of the line, from Coalville East to Shepshed, was on 11th December 1963. The station was demolished in 1974. Old Station Close was created on the trackbed and industrial units followed. The photo is from 22nd May 1965. (R.M.Casserley)

EAST OF SHEPSHED

Snells Nook

XVII.   The three halts were only served by steam railmotors. They ran on the line from 18th June 1906. No photo of one on the branch seems to exist. The upper part of this 1921 edition shows Garendon Deer Park. The drive to the Hall is marked with dotted lines. The squire had helped create the halt and golfers often used it.

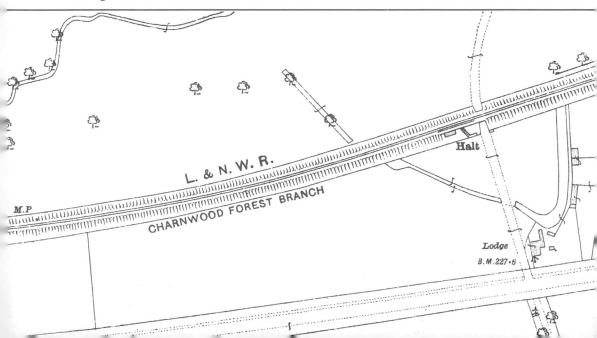

LOUGHBOROUGH DERBY ROAD

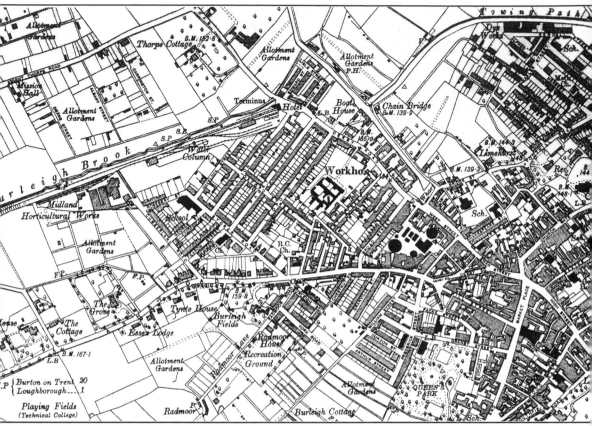

XVIII. The 1922 edition at 6ins to 1 mile includes a private siding on the left. In 1938, it was listed as Messenger's. Further east is the engine shed, water column and turntable. There was a 5-ton capacity crane.

51. A simple terminus was provided, with limited benefits such as a footwarmer filler and a W.H.Smith stall. A rare sight from a passenger platform was a weighted point lever. An Army ambulance train was based here during World War II. (R.M.Casserley coll.)

52.   The massive engine shed was closed in April 1931 and was later leased to a builders merchant, as was the goods shed. The engine is simply taking water; its train is seen in the next two pictures. (R.S.Carpenter coll.)

53.   Closure to passengers took place on 13th April 1931, but a tour appeared on 3rd May 1952. It is headed by class 2MT 2-6-2T no. 41218. It had started at Coventry and ran here via Shackerstone. It returned there by way of Ashby and Swadlincote. (R.S.Carpenter coll.)

54.   The same train is seen again. It is a push-pull set and had been pushed here. Hence the train could stand on the loop points, while the engine took water. The shed now stands in an industrial estate. Complete closure came on 31st October 1955. (R.S.Carpenter coll.)

55.   The station was inferior to the main two on the route. Even the station master had to use rented accommodation. A Morris Minor is seen in July 1952 on the side of the A6. A petrol filling station followed on the site, after demolition in 1965. Prior to that, the building had once served as a polling station, a rare joke to some. (J.Alsop coll.)

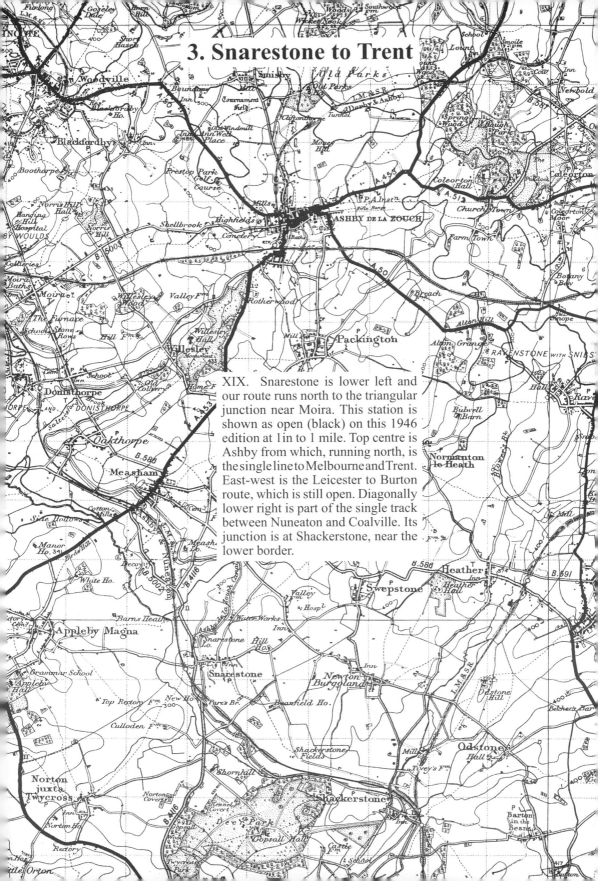

3. Snarestone to Trent

XIX. Snarestone is lower left and our route runs north to the triangular junction near Moira. This station is shown as open (black) on this 1946 edition at 1in to 1 mile. Top centre is Ashby from which, running north, is the single line to Melbourne and Trent. East-west is the Leicester to Burton route, which is still open. Diagonally lower right is part of the single track between Nuneaton and Coalville. Its junction is at Shackerstone, near the lower border.

SNARESTONE

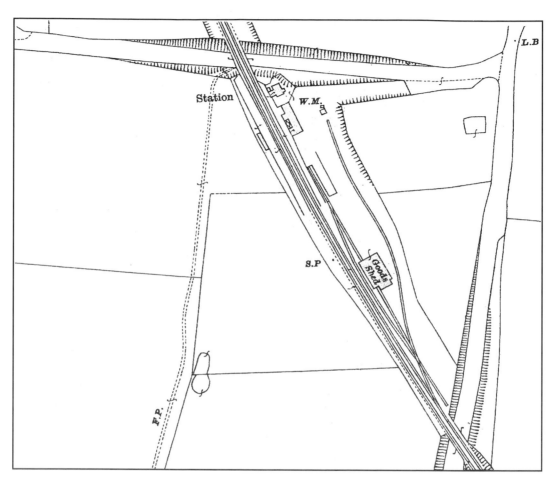

XX. The 1923 edition has the road to Appleby Magna on the left. Snarestone is just beyond the right border. It was the terminus of the Ashby Canal, after the northern part closed to traffic. The locals numbered 281 in 1901 and 329 in 1961.

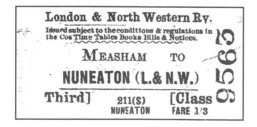

56. The station opened with the route on 1st September 1873 and is seen about 25 years later, complete with a bicycle. Many stations received telegrams and such devices were used for their delivery to the recipient, sometimes for an extra fee. In the foreground is a goods siding. (LOSA)

57. We can admire what was widely known as a 'running-in board' and can note that the facilities for gentlemen have no roof, a once common practice. The final E in the name was not always present in the early years. (LOSA)

58. Passenger trains ceased to call on 13th April 1931 and this is the scene on 27th October 1949. A few Summer excursion trains called here from about that time until 8th August 1961. (J.Alsop coll.)

59.   The road bridge details are revealed in the foreground in this fenceless view from 7th May 1961. On the right is the goods shed, which was fitted with a 30cwt crane. (M.J.Stretton coll.)

60.   A view from April 1965 includes the weigh house, on the right. Goods traffic continued here until 7th August 1967. Through goods trains continued until line closure in 1971. A ground frame sufficed. (R.S.Carpenter coll.)

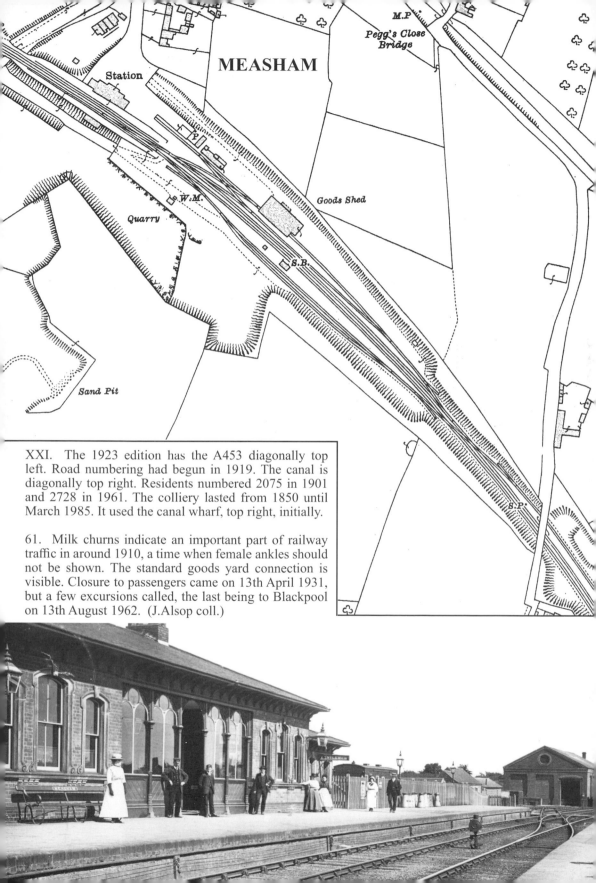

MEASHAM

Station

Pegg's Close
Bridge

M.P.

W.M.

Quarry

Goods Shed

S.B.

Sand Pit

S.P.

XXI. The 1923 edition has the A453 diagonally top left. Road numbering had begun in 1919. The canal is diagonally top right. Residents numbered 2075 in 1901 and 2728 in 1961. The colliery lasted from 1850 until March 1985. It used the canal wharf, top right, initially.

61. Milk churns indicate an important part of railway traffic in around 1910, a time when female ankles should not be shown. The standard goods yard connection is visible. Closure to passengers came on 13th April 1931, but a few excursions called, the last being to Blackpool on 13th August 1962. (J.Alsop coll.)

62.   The station approach was recorded on another postcard. The main building is in the distance, which was used for car repairs for many years. It was restored in 2007-08 to become the village museum. (P.Laming coll.)

63.   Working hard in April 1959 is no. 43679, a class 3F 0-6-0. It is seen from the bridge, lower right on the map, and is hauling coal from the despatch sidings. The colliery was east of the running lines, beyond the station. Sidings were added to the south, as seen. There were nine private sidings listed in 1938, four being on colliery land. (LOSA)

64.   Pictured in April 1965, the goods yard had been closed on 6th July 1964. The grain store is standing on staddle stones designed to keep out vermin. The shed was later used for boat building. (R.S.Carpenter coll.)

65.   The box had 35 levers and was in use from 1st April 1934 until 6th August 1972. The previous box here had opened in 1899. Colliery Sidings Box followed on 29th September 1902 and lasted until April 1934. The lines south of the colliery closed in 1971 and the route northwards to Moira Junction was singled, remaining in use until 1981. (M.A.King/R.Humm)

DONISTHORPE

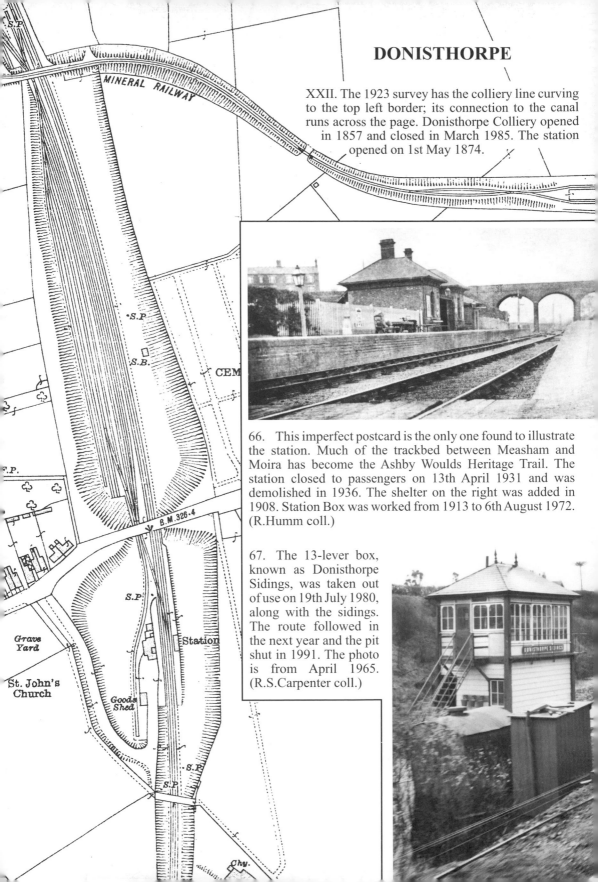

XXII. The 1923 survey has the colliery line curving to the top left border; its connection to the canal runs across the page. Donisthorpe Colliery opened in 1857 and closed in March 1985. The station opened on 1st May 1874.

66.   This imperfect postcard is the only one found to illustrate the station. Much of the trackbed between Measham and Moira has become the Ashby Woulds Heritage Trail. The station closed to passengers on 13th April 1931 and was demolished in 1936. The shelter on the right was added in 1908. Station Box was worked from 1913 to 6th August 1972. (R.Humm coll.)

67.   The 13-lever box, known as Donisthorpe Sidings, was taken out of use on 19th July 1980, along with the sidings. The route followed in the next year and the pit shut in 1991. The photo is from April 1965. (R.S.Carpenter coll.)

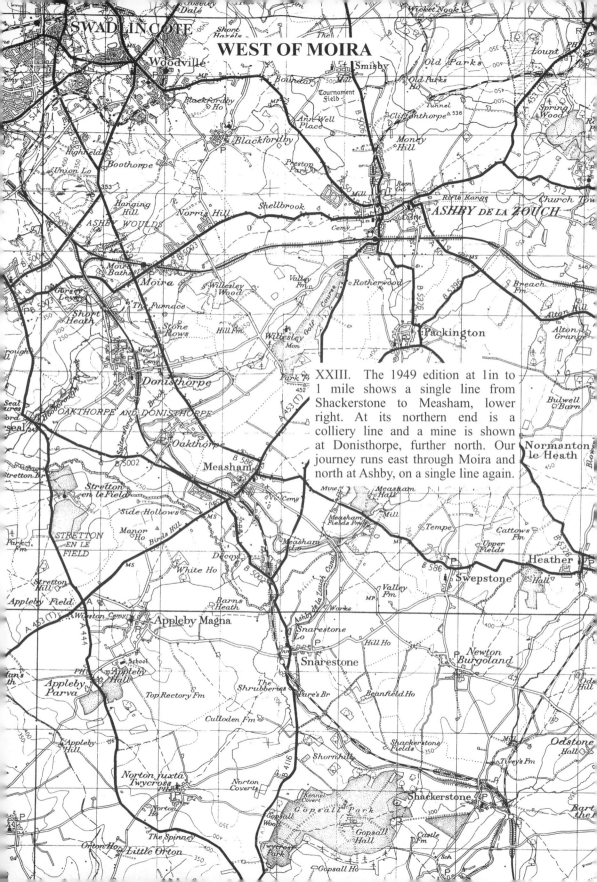

WEST OF MOIRA

XXIII. The 1949 edition at 1in to 1 mile shows a single line from Shackerstone to Measham, lower right. At its northern end is a colliery line and a mine is shown at Donisthorpe, further north. Our journey runs east through Moira and north at Ashby, on a single line again.

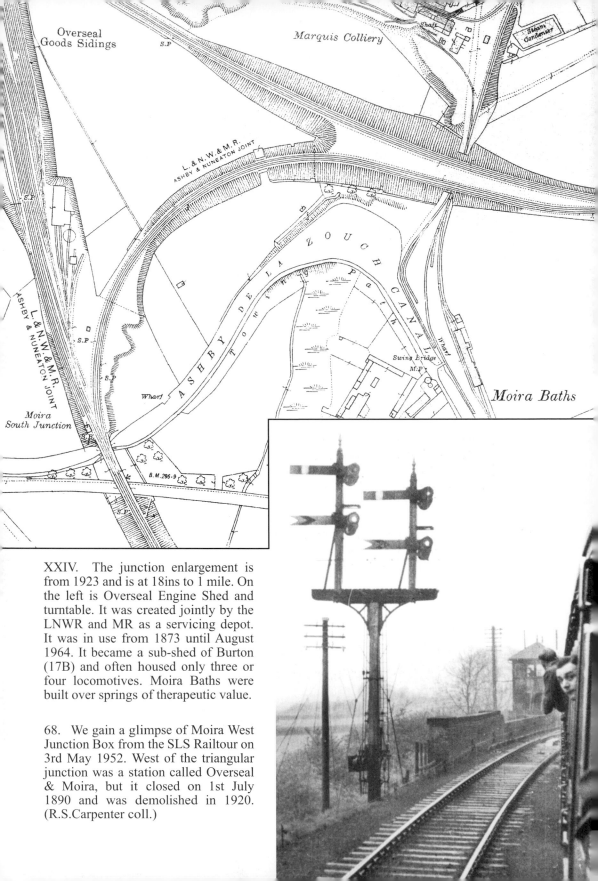

Overseal
Goods Sidings

Marquis Colliery

S.P

Steam
Condenser

Shaft

L. & N. W. & M. R.
ASHBY & NUNEATON JOINT

S.P.

A S H B Y   T o u c h   Z O U C H   C A N A L

Path

S.P.

Swing Bridge
M.P.

Wharf

L. & N. W. & M. R.
ASHBY & NUNEATON JOINT

S.P.

Wharf

Moira Baths

Moira
South Junction

B.M. 296·9

S.P.

XXIV. The junction enlargement is from 1923 and is at 18ins to 1 mile. On the left is Overseal Engine Shed and turntable. It was created jointly by the LNWR and MR as a servicing depot. It was in use from 1873 until August 1964. It became a sub-shed of Burton (17B) and often housed only three or four locomotives. Moira Baths were built over springs of therapeutic value.

68. We gain a glimpse of Moira West Junction Box from the SLS Railtour on 3rd May 1952. West of the triangular junction was a station called Overseal & Moira, but it closed on 1st July 1890 and was demolished in 1920. (R.S.Carpenter coll.)

MOIRA

69.   A westward view from 1949 has the junction in the distance and the small goods yard on the left. This was in use until 6th November 1963, while passengers were served from 1st March 1849 to 7th September 1964. (Stations UK)

> **Other views of this location can be seen in pictures 82 to 88 of the *Leicester to Burton* album.**

70.   Looking east in 1961, we find no platform canopies, but the essential signs are clear. No. 44085 is a class 4F 0-6-0 of MR design. There had been 15 private sidings listed near Moira in 1938, mostly for coal traffic. (Stations UK)

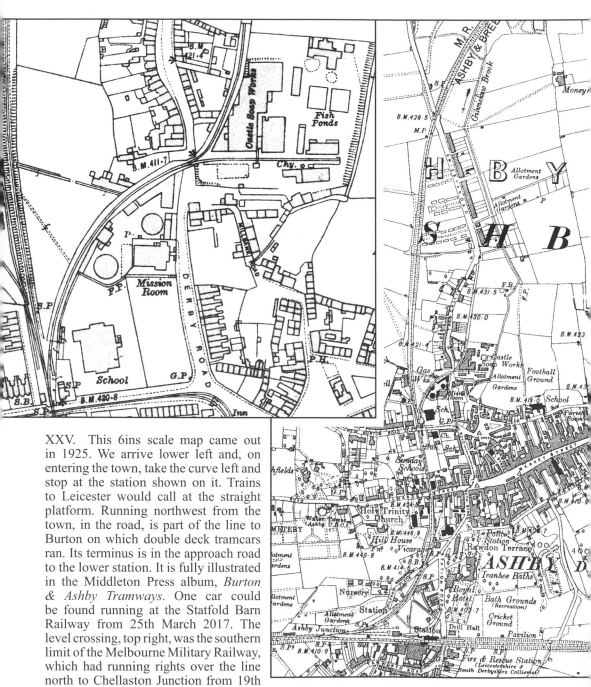

XXV. This 6ins scale map came out in 1925. We arrive lower left and, on entering the town, take the curve left and stop at the station shown on it. Trains to Leicester would call at the straight platform. Running northwest from the town, in the road, is part of the line to Burton on which double deck tramcars ran. Its terminus is in the approach road to the lower station. It is fully illustrated in the Middleton Press album, *Burton & Ashby Tramways*. One car could be found running at the Statfold Barn Railway from 25th March 2017. The level crossing, top right, was the southern limit of the Melbourne Military Railway, which had running rights over the line north to Chellaston Junction from 19th November 1939 until 1st January 1945. It served many Army stores and camps. Public service had been withdrawn on 22nd September 1930, but the Army moved local goods traffic during that war period. The line to the gas works (seen on the northern edge of the town and on the inset map) was open until 1964, but north thereof closed in 1955, as far as New Lount Colliery. This section ran through Ashby Tunnel. The Standard Soap Company had a siding beyond the gas works. The latter took 1500 tons of coal in 1900 and over 3000 tons in 1953.

71. Known as the Melbourne Branch platform, the curved one is seen on 22nd April 1951. The La Zouch family came to live here after the Norman invasion and their name lived on. The suffix was in use on the station from 1867, for a while, and was reinstated in 1924. The area is now occupied by housing. (J.Alsop coll.)

72. We look south towards the junction and its signal box. It had 28 levers and was worked from 1899 until 27th July 1964. Passengers could use the main station from 1st March 1849 until 7th September 1964. Freight was handled until 7th November 1963. (LOSA)

73. Two men are working the gates over Kilwarby Street, while those over Burton Road remain closed in the distance. On the right is the Methodist Chapel. This and the next three pictures were taken on 28th June 1952. (R.S.Carpenter coll.)

74. We move on to Burton Road crossing and look north to Holywell Mill. It was used by United Dairies in 1938. The box was in use from 1891 to 1931. (R.S.Carpenter coll.)

75. Further on we observe the stop blocks or scotch blocks on the track, which were controlled by rods from the hut. We are facing north as the staff and ticket for the SLS railtour are displayed. On the left are the remains of the Ticknall Wharf. The village was 3½ miles to the north. (R.S.Carpenter coll.)

Other views of this location can be found in *Leicester to Burton* in pictures 75 to 80.

76. We look northeast through the 308yd-long Ashby Tunnel. It was the former Ticknall Tramway tunnel. The tramway route dates from 1804 and was once a busy line that saw horse-drawn wagons transport limestone from Ticknall limeyards and quarries to canals in nearby Ashby-de-la-Zouch. It closed in stages up to 1913. (R.S.Carpenter coll.)

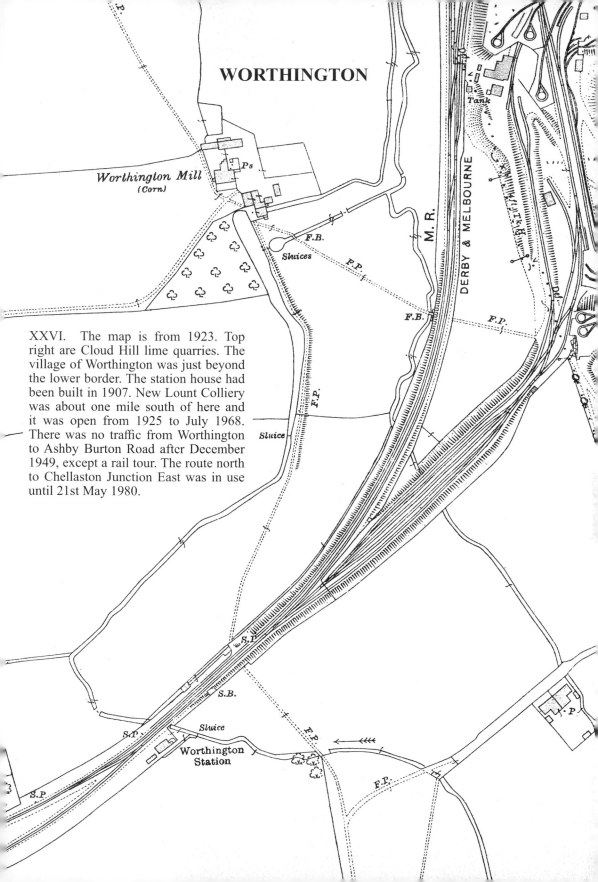

WORTHINGTON

Worthington Mill
(Corn)

Ps

F.B.

Sluices

F.P.

M. R.

DERBY & MELBOURNE

Tank

F.B.

F.P.

F.P.

Sluice

XXVI. The map is from 1923. Top right are Cloud Hill lime quarries. The village of Worthington was just beyond the lower border. The station house had been built in 1907. New Lount Colliery was about one mile south of here and it was open from 1925 to July 1968. There was no traffic from Worthington to Ashby Burton Road after December 1949, except a rail tour. The route north to Chellaston Junction East was in use until 21st May 1980.

S.B.

S.B.

S.P.

Sluice

F.P.

Worthington
Station

F.P.

S.P.

P

77.   A view northeast from 1949 includes a light frost on the single platform. It had not been used since 22nd September 1930, except by the Army in 1939-44. (R.M.Casserley coll.)

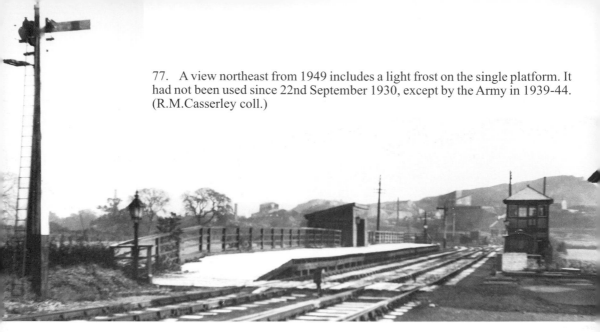

78.   The goods service to the single siding lasted until 7th May 1964. Ten private sidings were listed here or nearby in 1938. No train details remain. The 0-6-0 has LMS on its tender. The compartment stock may contain excursionists. (SLS coll.)

79.   The signal box had 12 levers and was in use from 1877 to 8th September 1968. It is seen on 12th May 1962, along with some of the extensive sidings for the limestone quarry. (R.M.Casserley)

TONGE & BREEDON

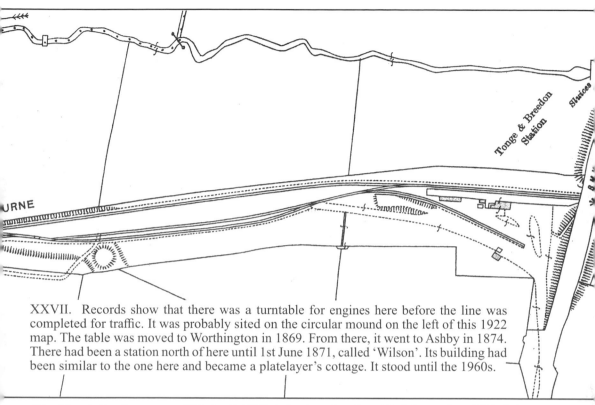

XXVII.   Records show that there was a turntable for engines here before the line was completed for traffic. It was probably sited on the circular mound on the left of this 1922 map. The table was moved to Worthington in 1869. From there, it went to Ashby in 1874. There had been a station north of here until 1st June 1871, called 'Wilson'. Its building had been similar to the one here and became a platelayer's cottage. It stood until the 1960s.

80.   The station is seen on 13th April 1952, it having closed on 22nd September 1930. It became a dwelling around 1970 and was later enlarged. Goods traffic ceased on 7th September 1959. In 1901, Tonge had 704 residents, this rising to 793 by 1961. BREEDON was added in 1897. (R.Humm coll.)

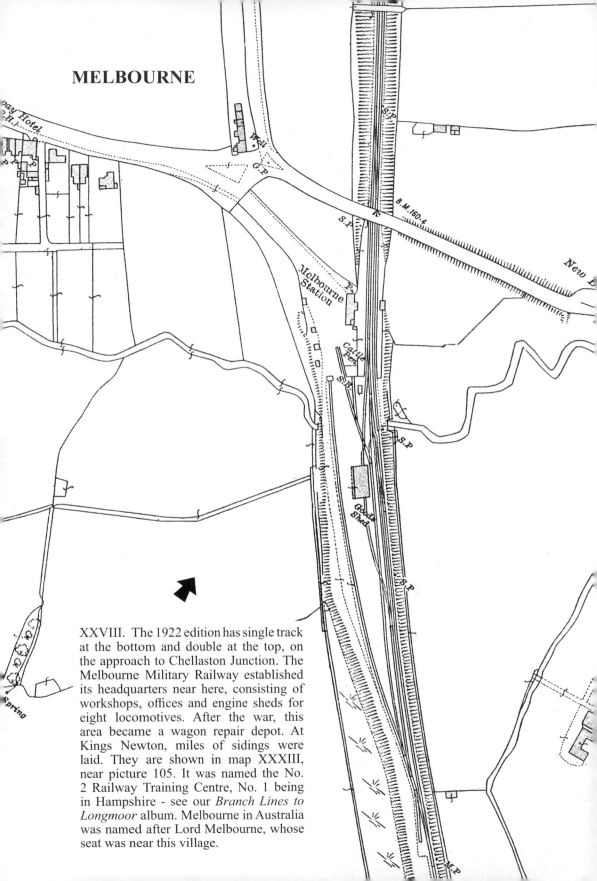

MELBOURNE

XXVIII. The 1922 edition has single track at the bottom and double at the top, on the approach to Chellaston Junction. The Melbourne Military Railway established its headquarters near here, consisting of workshops, offices and engine sheds for eight locomotives. After the war, this area became a wagon repair depot. At Kings Newton, miles of sidings were laid. They are shown in map XXXIII, near picture 105. It was named the No. 2 Railway Training Centre, No. 1 being in Hampshire - see our *Branch Lines to Longmoor* album. Melbourne in Australia was named after Lord Melbourne, whose seat was near this village.

81. A fine panorama was presented on a postcard in around 1900. The station was opened on 1st September 1868, the same day as the connection from Derby. It was a terminus for just 12 months. (J.Alsop coll.)

82. Seen on 1st April 1954 is no. 44087, a class 4F 0-6-0 returning empty coal wagons. Passenger service ceased on 22nd September 1930 and so the DMU is either on trial or on a special working. (A.G.Ellis/R.Humm)

83. The scene in 1965 includes evidence of its entire frontage. The goods yard had closed on 5th July 1964. The population was about 3600 from 1901 to 1931. The signal box had 20 levers and lasted from 1914 to 26th February 1967. (R.M.Casserley)

NORTH OF MELBOURNE

84. This is Kings Newton signal box, which had 15 levers and opened during World War II. We are looking towards Chellaston East Junction from the SLS Railtour on 28th June 1952. (R.S.Carpenter coll.)

85. Within minutes we are facing West Junction, with the Trent line on the right. The points were worked from a ground frame controlled by West Junction Box. (R.S.Carpenter coll.)

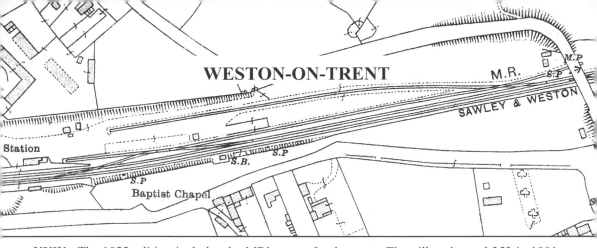

WESTON-ON-TRENT

M.R.

SAWLEY & WESTON

Station

Baptist Chapel

XXIX. The 1922 edition includes the MR's name for the route. The village housed 353 in 1901 and most were close to the station.

86. Four horse boxes make an unusual feature in the goods yard, as a westbound train approaches. The yard closed on 7th September 1959. It had no shed or crane. The station opened on 6th December 1869. (P.Laming coll.)

87. The Army built a suspension bridge over the River Trent here during the war to provide a link with Kings Newton for soldiers. This view from 15th April 1957 includes the weigh house, beyond the glass house, and the signal box, which had 16 levers. It was in use from 1898 to 24th April 1966. (Milepost 92½)

CASTLE DONINGTON & SHARDLOW

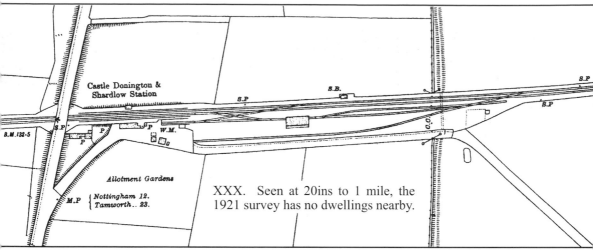

XXX. Seen at 20ins to 1 mile, the 1921 survey has no dwellings nearby.

88. This view east is from 13th April 1952 and is from the passenger crossing. The goods yard lasted until 1st May 1967 and there was a 30cwt crane inside the goods shed. The signal box was worked from April 1901 to 28th September 1969. (J.Alsop coll.)

89. Near the rear of the train is the signal box, which had 25 levers. The 5.30pm St. Pancras to Manchester Piccadilly was diverted on 22nd July 1962, due to electrification work on its usual route, but other details were not recorded. The yard seems busy. (M.J.Stretton coll.)

90. Apart from a missing chimney, all looked well in 1965, although there had been no passengers since 22nd September 1930. However, trains between Burton and Trent Junction were still speeding past in 2017. (R.M.Casserley)

91. Seen on 22nd May 1965, the buildings here were demolished in 1968. The platform edge had probably been removed just before the new flat-bottomed track was put in place. (R.M.Casserley)

92. Castle Donington Power Station has two photos from 16th April 1988. The Central Electricity Generating Board's Nos 1 and 2 are present with Merry-Go-Round wagons bringing in the coal. (T.Heavyside)

93.   No. 2 is seen again, together with the engine shed. Both nos 1 and 2 were Robert Stephenson & Hawthorns 0-4-0STs from 1954. Site construction began in 1951 and the first generator opened in 1958. However, they both closed in 1994. (T.Heavyside)

94.   Following demolition of the Power Station, Marks & Spencer built a distribution centre on the site. It opened on 8th May 2013 and its 900,000sq ft centre could handle online orders and store deliveries. The fully automated site will hold 16 million products and process a million items a day. There are 1200 people employed during peak periods. Its siding is single in the distance. Passing on 6th July 2013 is no. 60020, running from Westerleigh to Lindsey. (J.Whitehouse)

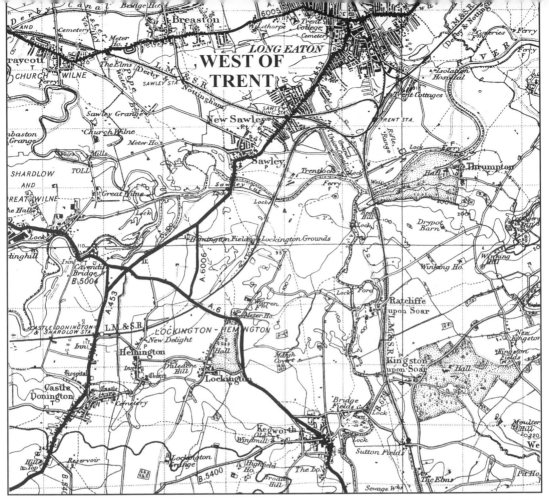

XXXI. The 1946 map at 2ins to 1 mile has our route lower left, the direct Derby line, top left, the Nottingham route, top right, and the main line, north-south. The next map gives more detail. The River Trent flows west to east and the River Soar runs north into it. The cuts can be studied.

95. We are just below the centre of the map with these two photographs. During the period of the WCML electrification in the early 1960s, certain London-Manchester trains were routed via Leicester, the Castle Donington route and Stoke-on-Trent. Class 5MT 4-6-0 no. 44966 and the Sunday 5.25pm St. Pancras-Manchester (Piccadilly) cross the River Trent for the second time, shortly after leaving Sheet Stores Junction on 26th June 1960. (M.J.Stretton coll.)

96. Close to Sawley Lock on 19th November 2011 were unusual visitors in the form of ex-GWR 0-6-0PTs nos L94 (ex.7752) and 9600. The tour was from, and back to, Tyseley Warwick Road, via Water Orton, Hinckley, Burton-on-Trent and Leicester, with 10 coaches forming the train. (J.Whitehouse)

97. We are approaching Sheet Stores Junction on 27th September 1959 behind ex-MR class 4P no. 1000. It had been repainted to appear thus. The train was to mark the Stephenson Locomotive Society's Golden Jubilee year. The box there had 36 levers and was closed on 28th September 1969. It was near to the Grand Union Canal bridge. The canals had a four-way junction at this location. (H.C.Casserley)

98. Lock Lane is ½ mile north of Trent Bridge and is seen on 29th April 1969. The 20-lever box was in use until that day. Lifting barriers under CCTV soon followed.
(H.B.Priestley/
R.Humm coll.)

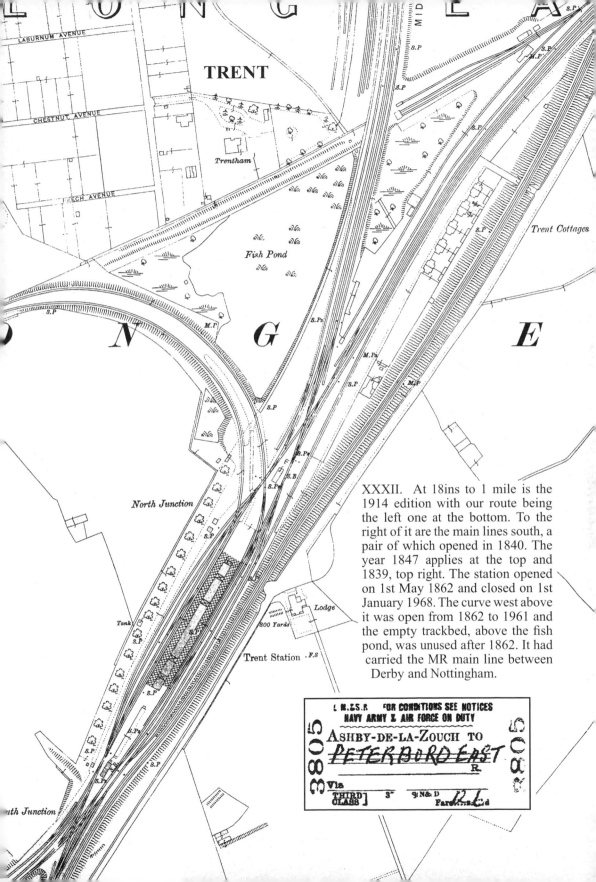

LONG EATON

TRENT

LABURNUM AVENUE

CHESTNUT AVENUE

BEECH AVENUE

Trentham

Fish Pond

Trent Cottages

MIDLAND

N G E

North Junction

Tank

800 Yards

Lodge

Trent Station · F.S

uth Junction

XXXII. At 18ins to 1 mile is the 1914 edition with our route being the left one at the bottom. To the right of it are the main lines south, a pair of which opened in 1840. The year 1847 applies at the top and 1839, top right. The station opened on 1st May 1862 and closed on 1st January 1968. The curve west above it was open from 1862 to 1961 and the empty trackbed, above the fish pond, was unused after 1862. It had carried the MR main line between Derby and Nottingham.

99. We are looking towards North Junction Box in about 1906. Access to the station was by way of a subway from the east side, at the north end. (J.Alsop coll.)

100. This is the down platform in the 1950s and the multitude of arches become visible. This was still an important place to change trains. Permissive working on some of the main lines here was allowed from 28th April 1940, due to the war. (J.F.Henton/R.Humm)

101. We gaze south at South Junction Box on 28th June 1952. It had a 68-lever frame. The gas lamp is of Sugg's Rochester pattern, which was free of shadows. The box closed on 26th May 1968. (R.S.Carpenter)

102. North Junction Box had a massive frame containing 75 levers and passing it on 3rd July 1965 is no. D1 *Scafell Pike*. The crossings are explained on the map. The box closed on 28th September 1969. The boxes were succeeded by one Power Box, which lasted until 9th July 2013, when East Midlands Control Centre took over. (H.B.Priestley/R.Humm)

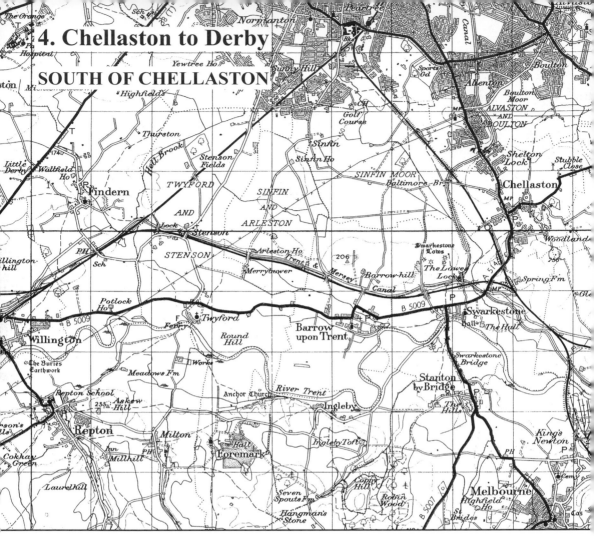

4. Chellaston to Derby

SOUTH OF CHELLASTON

XXXIII. The two junctions on the right of this 1949 extract at 1in to 1 mile are Chellaston East and West. Freight trains ceased to use the former in 1973 and the latter in 1980. The route east-west was still in use in 2017. King's Newton sidings appear lower right. Its signal box had 15 levers and was open from 1940 to 1962.

CHELLASTON & SWARKESTONE

103. This was initially the sole station on the route and it was opened on 1st September 1868. Here we look south in about 1900 with, probably, the entire staff, except the signalman. His box closed on 10th July 1966. There was a box at West Junction from 1901 to 1973. (R.Humm coll.)

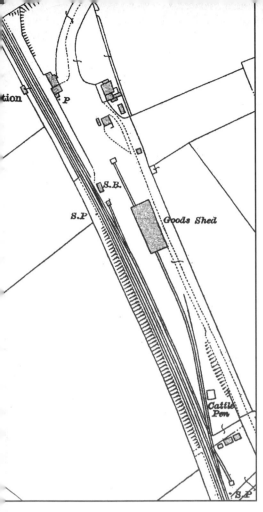

XXXIV. The 1922 survey shows a classical layout. A one ton crane was listed in 1938, but it does not appear here. The second name was added on 15th June 1901. Swarkestone housed 146 in 1901 and Chellaston had 645 souls.

104. Closure to passengers took place on 22nd September 1930, but all was still smart when photographed on 25th May 1957. Only the nameboard had gone; there were no seats to remove. A few excursions called in 1960-61. (Milepost 92½)

105. Many locomotives were stored here at the end of steam, awaiting the breaker's torch. This is the scene on 13th June 1966. The goods yard closed on 13th June 1966, but a few trains ran through until 1973. (J.Alsop coll.)

SINFIN CENTRAL

106. The original Sinfin sidings were opened on 2nd December 1921, but were closed by 1945. The line south of them was shut from 30th December 1973. A DMU is arriving from Derby on 17th March 1978. This station was largely for the benefit of Rolls Royce employees. Car production moved to Crewe in 1946, but other products continued. Both platforms were built for just three coaches. (R.Joanes)

107. The Rolls Royce private siding was photographed northwards on 14th February 1987. A typical train is to be seen in the next picture. Their car production business was sold and later moved to West Sussex. Aircraft components and parts for nuclear plants were among items made here. The oil deliveries serve the aeroengine test beds. (D.Birt/Midland Railway Study Centre)

SINFIN NORTH

108. Both Sinfin stations opened on 4th October 1976. They were built to convey staff to the developing industrial area; the main employers near here being Qualcast Ltd and International Combustion Ltd. It is 15th February 1987. The proposed extension to Chellaston did not come about and both stations closed on 17th May 1993, due to diminishing traffic. The platforms had to remain in place for 10 years in case conditions changed. There is now no trace. (D.Birt/Midland Railway Study Centre)

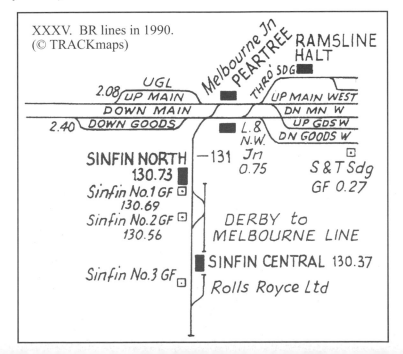

XXXV. BR lines in 1990.
(© TRACKmaps)

Melbourne Jn   RAMSLINE
PEARTREE   HALT
                THRO SDG

UGL
2.08 UP MAIN   UP MAIN WEST
      DOWN MAIN   DN MN W
2.40 DOWN GOODS   UP GDS W
                L.8   DN GOODS W
                N.W.

SINFIN NORTH   —131 Jn
130.73   0.75   S&T Sdg
Sinfin No.1 GF   GF 0.27
130.69
Sinfin No.2 GF   DERBY to
130.56   MELBOURNE LINE

                         SINFIN CENTRAL 130.37

Sinfin No.3 GF   Rolls Royce Ltd

109. No. 37711 comes off the Sinfin branch with the 12.35 Sinfin to Stanlow empty tank train on 8th July 1993. Both loaded and empty trains were routed via the Uttoxeter line and ran round at Derby. The flow switched to originating at Grangemouth refinery, after Stanlow stopped distributing its products by rail. It was still operating in 2017, using a weekly path via the East Coast main line. Also visible in the picture is a class 60-hauled steel train waiting in the up goods loop. There was a 36-lever signal box here from 1890 until 29th June 1969. There were local sidings on the left until 4th January 1965. Willington Power Station is in the background. (P.D.Shannon)

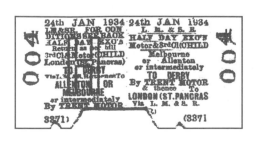

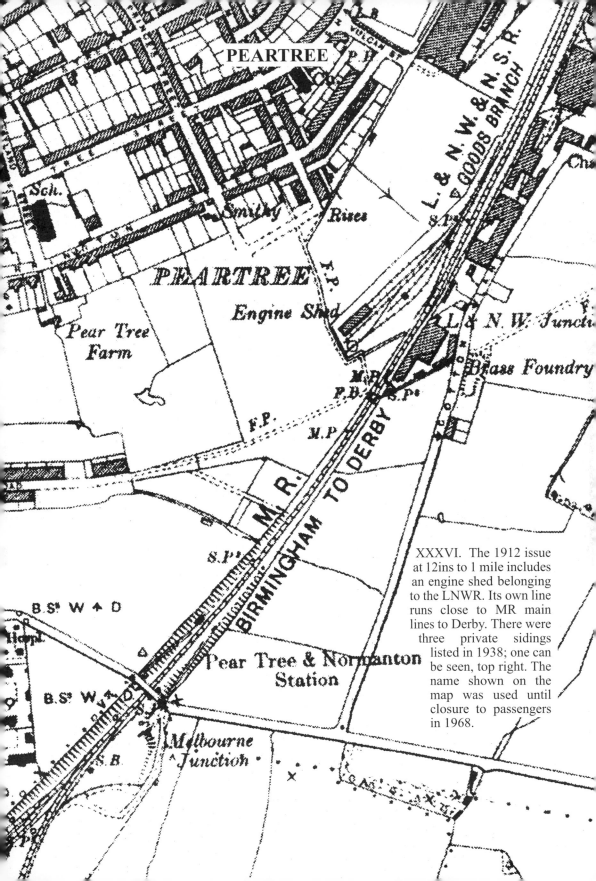

PEARTREE

VULCAN ST

L. & N. W. & N. S. R.
GOODS BRANCH

Ch___

Sch.

Smithy   Rises

PEARTREE   F.P.

Engine Shed   L & N. W. Junctio___

Pear Tree
Farm

                                        Brass Foundry

                    M.B.
                    P.B.   S.P.

F.P.
        M.P.

M. R.

BIRMINGHAM TO DERBY

S.P.

B S⁺ W ↟ D

Hos___

Pear Tree & Normanton
Station

B S⁺ W

S.B.

Melbourne
Junction

XXXVI. The 1912 issue at 12ins to 1 mile includes an engine shed belonging to the LNWR. Its own line runs close to MR main lines to Derby. There were three private sidings listed in 1938; one can be seen, top right. The name shown on the map was used until closure to passengers in 1968.

110. This ex-MR class 1F, outside-framed, 0-6-0 is northbound in 1923 with mixed freight. It is LMS no. 2687. Its springs could be easily lubricated. The ticket office is in the steam above the first wagon. (P.Laming coll.)

111. It is 1st February 1958 and we can see class 5MT 2-6-0 no. 42799 working hard with an empty stock train. Closure to passengers took place on 4th March 1968, but it was reopened on 4th October 1976, as just Peartree. The paths to the platform are behind the fences. By May 1993, the service on offer comprised trains arriving from Matlock at 06.48 and 07.33 and a departure to there at 07.01, plus a 16.26 to Nottingham, weekdays only. (Milepost 92½)

112. The first station was north of the one now in use. It closed on 10th May 1840, having opened on 12th August 1839. The spacious facility was fitted with long smoke hoods to reduce coughing and spitting. Derby West ticket platform was in use until 1st December 1900. (J.Alsop coll.)

113. Seen on 27th December 1926 is MR no. 85, a 2-4-0 of class 1P. The hose support is seen in action in the next picture. Gas for the lamps and the town was produced adjacent to the eastern border of the works, but not by the railways. They removed the coke and tar, but the coal mostly came in canal barges. (H.C.Casserley)

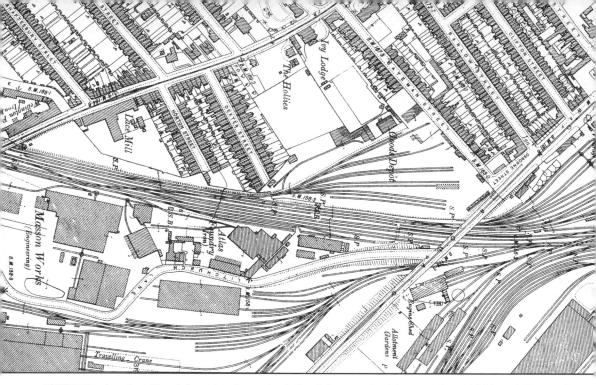

XXXVII. London Road Junction is to the left of the gap in this map from 1900 at 15ins to 1 mile. Only part of the massive Derby Works of the MR is shown. The shaded circles indicate engine round houses, used largely for operational locomotives. We arrive on one of the lines in the upper left group. The upper one had a platform called Ramsline Halt, but it was only used in 1990, for football traffic. Note that there are two footbridges; both for staff only. *[continued overleaf...]*

114. It is now 13th July 1947 and at the south end of the station is no. 2361, an LMS class 4P 2-6-4T. At the foot of the water column is a brazier used to prevent freezing. Parcels abound. A rare air raid had damaged platform 6 on 15th January 1941, killing six. (H.C.Casserley)

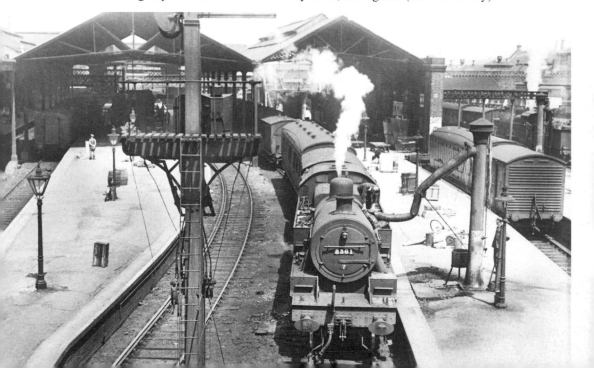

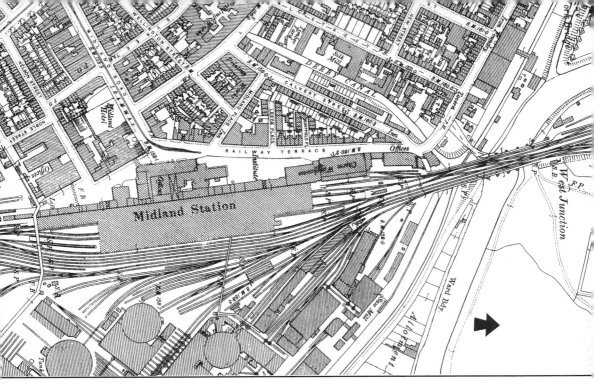

[...continued from overleaf] The main line from Nottingham is in the group at the lower border of the left page. Rails are in some streets. Electric trams ran from 1904 to 1934 and trolleybuses were used in 1932-67. Some of the many signal boxes are shown. Simplification came on 29th August 2008, when the new East Midlands Control Centre opened, located just west of London Road Junction.

115. This northward panorama in 1954 was recorded during the total rebuilding of all platform structures, including 'A' Box. All the components seen were of precast concrete. The final steam engine to be built in Derby Works left on 14th June 1957. (Stations UK)

→ 116. Seen in about 1963 is 'Jubilee' class 4-6-0 no. 45685 *Barfleur*, with a trio of admirers. Modern electric lighting had been included in the rebuild. The term MIDLAND was in use from 25th September 1950 to 6th May 1968, officially. Derby Friargate station had closed on 5th September 1964. (Stations UK)

117. This splendid western facade featured the entrance and was in use from 1891. It replaced a featureless structure, which failed to show the importance of the MR. The photo is from 15th August 1983. (R.J.Buckley/Initial Photographics)

118. The fine structure just seen was demolished in 1985 and only a few parts were taken for use elsewhere. A spacious new booking hall was created with easy access to all the platforms. The exterior was given the word 'Midland', although not widely used, plus an MR coat of arms. (R.Humm coll.)

XXXVIII. The BR track diagram is from 1990 and marks the route from Peartree as Up Main West from Birmingham. (© TRACKmaps)

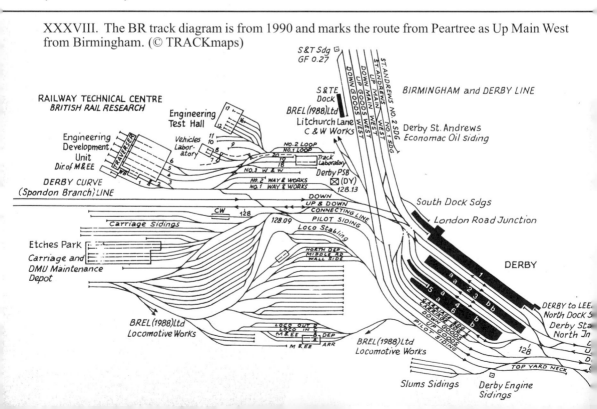

119. This and the next view are dated 10th October 2015. They are intended to give a broad view north and then one south. Staff had a superior footbridge, but the early offices were retained on the right, together with the tower, which had a clock and a bell. Shunting empty to the depot is no. 222013. The Works had marked its 175th anniversary of opening on 15th May 2014. (V.Mitchell)

A more extensive coverage can be found in pictures 84 to 120 in our *Tamworth to Derby* **album. Middleton Press have also produced** *Derby Tramways,* *Derby to Stoke-on-Trent* **and** *Derby to Chesterfield.*

120. We can enjoy an uncluttered panorama from the bay platform. In attendance, but idle, are nos 20118, 20132, 20314 and 20107, plus two barrier wagons. An excellent service was provided from here to all points of the compass. (V.Mitchell)

MP Middleton Press

EVOLVING THE ULTIMATE RAIL ENCYCLOPEDIA

Easebourne Midhurst GU29 9AZ. Tel:01730 813169

www.middletonpress.co.uk email:info@middletonpress.co.uk
A-978 0 906520 B- 978 1 873793 C- 978 1 901706 D-978 1 904474
E - 978 1 906008 F - 978 1 908174 G - 978 1 910356

All titles listed below were in print at time of publication - please check current availability by looking at our website - *www.middletonpress.co.uk* or by requesting a Brochure which includes our *LATEST* RAILWAY TITLES also our TRAMWAY, TROLLEYBUS, MILITARY and COASTAL series

A
Abergavenny to Merthyr C 91 8
Abertillery & Ebbw Vale Lines D 84 5
Aberystwyth to Carmarthen E 90 1
Allhallows - Branch Line to A 62 8
Alton - Branch Lines to A 11 6
Andover to Southampton A 82 6
Ascot - Branch Lines around A 64 2
Ashburton - Branch Line to B 95 4
Ashford - Steam to Eurostar B 67 1
Ashford to Dover A 48 2
Austrian Narrow Gauge D 04 3
Avonmouth - BL around D 42 5
Aylesbury to Rugby D 91 3

B
Baker Street to Uxbridge D 90 6
Bala to Llandudno E 87 1
Banbury to Birmingham D 27 2
Banbury to Cheltenham E 63 5
Bangor to Holyhead F 01 7
Bangor to Portmadoc E 72 7
Barking to Southend C 80 2
Barmouth to Pwllheli E 53 6
Barry - Branch Lines around D 50 0
Bartlow - Branch Lines to F 27 7
Barton-on-Humber - BL to G 09 8 6
Bath Green Park to Bristol C 36 9
Bath to Evercreech Junction A 60 4
Beamish 40 years on rails E94 9
Bedford to Wellingborough D 31 9
Berwick to Drem F 64 2
Berwick to St. Boswells F 75 8
B'ham to Tamworth & Nuneaton F 63 5
Birkenhead to West Kirby F 61 1
Birmingham to Wolverhampton E253
Blackburn to Hellifield F 95 6
Bletchley to Cambridge D 94 4
Bletchley to Rugby E 07 9
Bodmin - Branch Lines around B 83 1
Boston to Lincoln F 80 2
Bournemouth to Evercreech Jn A 46 8
Bournemouth to Weymouth A 57 4
Bradshaw's History F18 5
Bradshaw's Rail Times 1850 F 13 0
Bradshaw's Rail Times 1895 F 11 6
Branch Lines series - see town names
Brecon to Neath D 43 2
Brecon to Newport D 16 6
Brecon to Newtown E 06 2
Brighton to Eastbourne A 16 1
Brighton to Worthing A 03 1
Bristol to Taunton D 03 6
Bromley South to Rochester B 23 7
Bromsgrove to Birmingham D 87 6
Bromsgrove to Gloucester D 73 9
Broxbourne to Cambridge F16 1
Brunel - A railtour D 74 6
Bude - Branch Line to B 29 9
Burnham to Evercreech Jn B 68 0

C
Cambridge to Ely D 55 5
Canterbury - BLs around B 58 9
Cardiff to Dowlais (Cae Harris) E 47 5
Cardiff to Pontypridd E 95 6
Cardiff to Swansea E 42 0
Carlisle to Hawick E 85 7
Carmarthen to Fishguard E 66 6
Caterham & Tattenham Corner B251
Central & Southern Spain NG E 91 8
Chard and Yeovil - BLs a C 30 7
Charing Cross to Dartford A 75 8
Charing Cross to Orpington A 96 3
Cheddar - Branch Line to B 90 9
Cheltenham to Andover C 43 7
Cheltenham to Redditch D 81 4
Chester to Birkenhead F 21 5
Chester to Manchester F 51 2
Chester to Rhyl E 93 2
Chester to Warrington F 40 6
Chichester to Portsmouth A 14 7
Clacton and Walton - BLs to F 04 8
Clapham Jn to Beckenham Jn B 36 7
Cleobury Mortimer - BLs a E 18 5
Clevedon & Portishead - BLs to D180
Consett to South Shields E 57 4
Cornwall Narrow Gauge D 56 2
Corris and Vale of Rheidol E 65 9
Coventry to Leicester G 00 5
Craven Arms to Llandeilo E 35 2
Craven Arms to Wellington E 33 8
Crawley to Littlehampton A 34 5
Crewe to Manchester F 57 4
Cromer - Branch Lines around C 26 0
Croydon to East Grinstead B 48 0
Crystal Palace & Catford Loop B 87 1
Cyprus Narrow Gauge E 13 0

D
Darjeeling Revisited F 09 3
Darlington Leamside Newcastle E 28 4
Darlington to Newcastle D 98 2
Dartford to Sittingbourne B 34 3
Denbigh - Branch Lines around F 32 1
Derby to Stoke-on-Trent F 93 2
Derwent Valley - BL to the D 06 7
Devon Narrow Gauge E 09 3
Didcot to Banbury D 02 9
Didcot to Swindon C 84 0
Didcot to Winchester C 13 0
Dorset & Somerset NG D 76 0
Douglas - Laxey - Ramsey E 75 8
Douglas to Peel C 88 8
Douglas to Port Erin C 55 0
Douglas to Ramsey D 39 5
Dover to Ramsgate A 78 9
Drem to Edinburgh G 06 7
Dublin Northwards in 1950s E 31 4
Dunstable - Branch Lines to E 27 7

E
Ealing to Slough C 42 0
Eastbourne to Hastings A 27 7
East Cornwall Mineral Railways D 22 7
East Croydon to Three Bridges A 53 6
Eastern Spain Narrow Gauge E 56 7
East Grinstead - BLs to A 07 9
East Kent Light Railway A 61 1
East London - Branch Lines of C 44 4
East London Line B 80 0
East of Norwich - Branch Lines E 69 7
Effingham Junction - BLs a A 74 1
Ely to Norwich C 90 1
Enfield Town & Palace Gates D 32 6
Epsom to Horsham A 30 7
Eritrean Narrow Gauge E 38 3
Euston to Harrow & Wealdstone C 89 5
Exeter to Barnstaple B 15 2
Exeter to Newton Abbot C 49 9
Exeter to Tavistock B 69 5
Exmouth - Branch Lines to B 00 8

F
Fairford - Branch Line to A 52 9
Falmouth, Helston & St. Ives C 74 1
Fareham to Salisbury A 67 3
Faversham to Dover B 05 3
Felixstowe & Aldeburgh - BL to D 20 3
Fenchurch Street to Barking C 20 8
Festiniog - 50 yrs of enterprise C 83 3
Festiniog 1946-55 E 01 7
Festiniog in the Fifties B 68 8
Festiniog in the Sixties B 91 6
Ffestiniog in Colour 1955-82 F 25 3
Finsbury Park to Alexandra Pal C 02 8
French Metre Gauge Survivors F 88 8
Frome to Bristol B 77 0

G
Galashiels to Edinburgh F 52 9
Gloucester to Bristol D 35 7
Gloucester to Cardiff D 66 1
Gosport - Branch Lines around A 36 9
Greece Narrow Gauge D 72 2

H
Hampshire Narrow Gauge D 36 4
Harrow to Watford D 14 2
Harwich & Hadleigh - BLs to F 02 4
Harz Revisited F 62 8
Hastings to Ashford A 37 6
Hawick to Galashiels F 36 9
Hawkhurst - Branch Line to A 66 6
Hayling - Branch Line to A 12 3
Hay-on-Wye - BL around D 92 0
Haywards Heath to Seaford A 28 4
Hemel Hempstead - BLs to D 88 3
Henley, Windsor & Marlow - BLa C77 2
Hereford to Newport D 54 8
Hertford & Hatfield - BLs a E 58 1
Hertford Loop E 71 0
Hexham to Carlisle D 75 3
Hexham to Hawick F 08 6
Hitchin to Peterborough D 07 4
Holborn Viaduct to Lewisham A 81 9
Horsham - Branch Lines to A 02 4
Huntingdon - Branch Line to A 93 2

I
Ilford to Shenfield C 97 0
Ilfracombe - Branch Line to B 21 3
Industrial Rlys of the South East A 09 3
Ipswich to Diss F 81 9
Ipswich to Saxmundham C 41 3
Isle of Man Railway Journey F 94 9
Isle of Wight Lines - 50 yrs C 12 3
Italy Narrow Gauge F 17 8

K
Kent Narrow Gauge C 45 1
Kettering to Nottingham F 82-6
Kidderminster to Shrewsbury E 10 9
Kingsbridge - Branch Line to C 98 7
Kings Cross to Potters Bar E 62 8
King's Lynn to Hunstanton F 58 1
Kingston & Hounslow Loops A 83 3
Kingswear - Branch Line to C 17 8

L
Lambourn - Branch Line to C 70 3
Launceston & Princetown - BLs C 19 2
Leek - Branch Line From G 01 2
Leicester to Burton F 85 7
Lewisham to Dartford A 92 5
Lincoln to Cleethorpes F 56 7
Lincoln to Doncaster G 03 6
Lines around Stamford F 98 7
Lines around Wimbledon B 75 6
Liverpool Street to Chingford D 01 2
Liverpool Street to Ilford C 34 5
Llandeilo to Swansea E 46 8
London Bridge to Addiscombe B 20 6
London Bridge to East Croydon A 58 1
Longmoor - Branch Lines to A 41 3
Looe - Branch Line to C 22 2
Loughborough to Nottingham F 68 0
Lowestoft - BLs around E 40 6
Ludlow to Hereford E 14 7
Lydney - Branch Lines around E 26 0
Lyme Regis - Branch Line to A 45 1
Lynton - Branch Line to B 04 6

M
Machynlleth to Barmouth E 54 3
Maesteg and Tondu Lines E 06 2
Majorca & Corsica Narrow Gauge F 41 3
March - Branch Lines around B 09 1
Market Drayton - BLs around F 67 3
Market Harborough to Newark F 86 4
Marylebone to Rickmansworth D 49 4
Melton Constable to Yarmouth Bch E031
Midhurst - Branch Lines of E 78 9
Midhurst - Branch Lines to F 00 0
Minehead - Branch Line to A 80 2
Mitcham Junction Lines B 01 5
Monmouth - Branch Lines to E 20 8
Monmouthshire Eastern Valleys D 71 5
Moretonhampstead - BL to C 27 7
Moreton-in-Marsh to Worcester D 26 5
Morpeth to Bellingham F 87 1
Mountain Ash to Neath D 80 7

N
Newark to Doncaster F 78 9
Newbury to Westbury C 66 6
Newcastle to Hexham D 69 2
Newport (IOW) - Branch Lines to A 26 0
Newquay - Branch Lines to C 71 0
Newton Abbot to Plymouth C 60 4
Newtown to Aberystwyth E 41 3
Northampton to Peterborough F 92 5
North East German NG D 44 9
Northern Alpine Narrow Gauge F 37 6
Northern France Narrow Gauge C 75 8
Northern Spain Narrow Gauge E 83 3
North London Line B 94 7
North of Birmingham F 55 0
North Woolwich - BLs around C 65 9
Nottingham to Boston F 70 3
Nottingham to Lincoln F 43 7
Nuneaton to Loughborough G 08 1

O
Ongar - Branch Line to E 05 5
Orpington to Tonbridge B 03 9
Oswestry - Branch Lines around E 60 4
Oswestry to Whitchurch E 81 9
Oxford to Bletchley D 57 9
Oxford to Moreton-in-Marsh D 15 9

P
Paddington to Ealing C 37 6
Paddington to Princes Risborough C819
Padstow - Branch Line to B 54 1
Pembroke and Cardigan - BLs to F 29 1
Peterborough to Kings Lynn E 32 1
Peterborough to Lincoln F 89 5
Peterborough to Newark F 72 7
Plymouth - BLs around B 98 5
Plymouth to St. Austell C 63 5
Pontypool to Mountain Ash D 65 4
Pontypridd to Merthyr F 14 7
Pontypridd to Port Talbot E 86 4
Porthmadog 1954-94 - BLa B 31 2
Portmadoc 1923-46 - BLa B 13 8
Portsmouth to Southampton A 31 4
Portugal Narrow Gauge E 67 3
Potters Bar to Cambridge D 70 8
Princes Risborough - BL to D 05 0
Princes Risborough to Banbury C 85 7

R
Railways to Victory C 16 1
Reading to Basingstoke B 27 5
Reading to Didcot C 79 6
Reading to Guildford A 47 5
Redhill to Ashford A 73 4
Return to Blaenau 1970-82 C 64 2
Rhyl to Bangor F 15 4
Rhymney & New Tredegar Lines E 48 2
Rickmansworth to Aylesbury D 61 6
Romania & Bulgaria NG E 23 9
Romneyrail C 32 1
Ross-on-Wye - BLs around E 30 7
Ruabon to Barmouth E 84 0
Rugby to Birmingham E 37 6
Rugby to Loughborough F 12 3
Rugby to Stafford F 07 9
Rugeley to Stoke-on-Trent F 90 1
Ryde to Ventnor A 19 2

S
Salisbury to Westbury B 39 8
Sardinia and Sicily Narrow Gauge F 50 5
Saxmundham to Yarmouth C 69 7
Saxony & Baltic Germany Revisited F 71 0
Saxony Narrow Gauge D 47 0
Seaton & Sidmouth - BLs to A 95 6
Selsey - Branch Line to A 04 8
Sheerness - Branch Line to B 16 2
Shenfield to Ipswich E 96 3
Shrewsbury - Branch Line to A 86 4
Shrewsbury to Chester E 70 3
Shrewsbury to Crewe F 48 2
Shrewsbury to Ludlow E 21 5
Shrewsbury to Newtown E 29 1
Sierra Leone Narrow Gauge D 28 9
Sirhowy Valley Line E 12 3
Sittingbourne to Ramsgate A 90 1
Skegness & Mablethorpe - BL to F 84 0
Slough to Newbury C 56 7
South African Two-foot gauge E 51 2
Southampton to Bournemouth A 42 0
Southend & Southminster BLs E 76 5
Southern Alpine Narrow Gauge F 22 2
Southern France Narrow Gauge C 47 5
South London Line B 46 6
South Lynn to Norwich City F 03 1
Southwold - Branch Line to A 15 4
Spalding - Branch Lines around E 52 9
Spalding to Grimsby F 65 9 6
Stafford to Chester F 34 5
Stafford to Wellington F 59 8
St Albans to Bedford D 08 1
St. Austell to Penzance C 67 3
St. Boswell to Berwick F 44 4
Steaming Through Isle of Wigh
Steaming Through West Hants
Stourbridge to Wolverhampton
St. Pancras to Barking D 68 5
St. Pancras to Folkestone E 88
St. Pancras to St. Albans C 78
Stratford to Cheshunt F 53 6
Stratford-u-Avon to Birminghar
Stratford-u-Avon to Cheltenhar
Sudbury - Branch Lines to F 1
Surrey Narrow Gauge C 87 1
Sussex Narrow Gauge C 68 0
Swaffham - Branch Lines arou
Swanage to 1999 - BL to A 33
Swanley to Ashford B 45 9
Swansea - Branch Lines arour
Swansea to Carmarthen E 59
Swindon to Bristol C 96 3
Swindon to Gloucester D 46 3
Swindon to Newport D 30 2
Swiss Narrow Gauge C 94 9

T
Talyllyn 60 E 98 7
Tamworth to Derby F 76 5
Taunton to Barnstaple B 60 2
Taunton to Exeter C 82 6
Taunton to Minehead F 39 0
Tavistock to Plymouth B 88 6
Tenterden - Branch Line to A 2
Three Bridges to Brighton A 3
Tilbury Loop C 86 4
Tiverton - BLs around C 62 8
Tivetshall to Beccles D 41 8
Tonbridge to Hastings A 44 4
Torrington - Branch Lines to B
Tourist Railways of France G (
Towcester - BLs around E 39
Tunbridge Wells BLs A 32 1

U
Upwell - Branch Line to B 64
Uttoxeter to Macclesfield G 0

V
Victoria to Bromley South A 9
Victoria to East Croydon A 40
Vivarais Revisited E 08 6

W
Walsall Routes F 45 1
Wantage - Branch Line to D 2
Wareham to Swanage 50 yrs
Waterloo to Windsor A 54 3
Waterloo to Woking A 38 3
Watford to Leighton Buzzard
Wellingborough to Leicester F
Welshpool to Llanfair E 49 9
Wenford Bridge to Fowey C 0
Westbury to Bath B 55 8
Westbury to Taunton C 76 5
West Cornwall Mineral Rlys D
West Croydon to Epsom B 08
West German Narrow Gauge
West London - BLs of C 50 5
West London Line B 84 8
West Wiltshire - BLs of D 12
Weymouth - BLs A 65 9
Willesden Jn to Richmond B
Wimbledon to Beckenham C
Wimbledon to Epsom B 62 6
Wimborne - BLs around A 97
Wisbech - BLs around C 01 7
Witham & Kelvedon - BLs a E
Woking to Alton A 59 8
Woking to Portsmouth A 25 3
Woking to Southampton A 55
Wolverhampton to Shrewsbu
Wolverhampton to Stafford F
Worcester to Birmingham D 9
Worcester to Hereford D 38 8
Worthing to Chichester A 06
Wrexham to New Brighton F
Wroxham - BLs around F 31

Y
Yeovil - 50 yrs change C 38 3
Yeovil to Dorchester A 76 5
Yeovil to Exeter A 91 8
York to Scarborough F 23 9